ABHANDLUNGEN ZUR KUNST-, MUSIK- UND
LITERATURWISSENSCHAFT, BAND 163

Dialectical Humor in Hermann Kant's Novel "Die Aula"

A STUDY IN CONTEMPORARY EAST GERMAN LITERATURE

BY THEODOR LANGENBRUCH

1975

BOUVIER VERLAG HERBERT GRUNDMANN · BONN

To my wife

CIP-Kurztitelaufnahme der Deutschen Bibliothek
LANGENBRUCH, THEODOR
Dialectical humor in Hermann Kant's novel 'Die Aula':
a study in contemporary East German literature.
(Abhandlungen zur Kunst-, Musik- und Literaturwissenschaft; Bd. 163)
ISBN 3-416-00993-2

CONTENTS

INTRODUCTION

Hermann Kant's first novel *Die Aula* was published in book form in 1965, and acclaimed in both East and West Germany as one of the major literary contributions of the decade. The plot of the *Aula* is simple: Robert Iswall, valedictorian of the first graduating class of the "Workers' and Peasants' College" at Greifswald, is asked by his former dean to deliver the convocation speech at the closing of the college which, in a span of thirteen years, has fulfilled its historical mission. The gathering of material for this speech constitutes the framework of the novel, into which a wide variety of anecdotes, small episodes, and reflective passages are fitted. Thus the *Aula* becomes an anecdotal chronicle of developments in East Germany since World War II.

Indeed, developments did take place in East Germany after the war, and also the literary scene underwent radical changes. It is difficult to agree on any one assessment of literary development in East Germany. However, some background information concerning conditions and circumstances under which literature is written and read there is indispensable for any study of East German literature. Therefore, before turning to Kant's *Aula*, I would like to briefly outline some aspects of the novel's environment. I hope that the material presented here will prove helpful in deepening understanding of both East German literature as a whole and of Hermann Kant's *Aula*, in particular.

The following episode capsules the situation of literature in East Germany, and also spotlights Kant's own position of critical involvement. On January 14, 1971, East German Chairman Walter Ulbricht had a "discussion of ideas" ("Ideenberatung") in the State Council with authors and performing artists. In his opening words, Ulbricht mentioned among other things "new conflicts"; he pointed out that these new conflicts consisted mainly in bourgeois and petit-bourgeois habits not being overcome just by peaceful discussions, but sometimes having to be overcome through hard argumentation at the job, in the family, or in Party organizations. Ulbricht furthermore demanded the conquering of mediocrity in the struggle to solve these "new conflicts," and spoke further of the necessity of looking at the present situation from the vantage

1

point of the future. In the ensuing discussion, Kant referred to Ulbricht's own words of the "new conflicts" by saying that, as an author, "one should keep in mind that one should cause no harm with what one writes"; "however," he added, "it is to be questioned whether one actually does harm when one writes about things that are difficult." With this, Kant was probably alluding to his second novel *Das Impressum* which was barred from publication for two years, being published only in Spring 1972. Ulbricht's response to Kant's questioning speaks for itself: "Comrade Kant has helped us find the crucial link in the chain by saying that what matters is to write about difficult things in such a way that they do no harm to society's development. However, that is not the whole truth. The whole truth is that the literary work must not only do no harm to our socialist society, but it must also help in the development of socialist personalities."[1]

In East Germany, a writer is regarded as an integral part of his socialist society, with all the consequences this entails. Authors are granted privileges and financial support; a host of literary activities are sponsored. In brief, literature enjoys publicity and recognition unparalleled in western countries. On the other hand, a socialist society has certain demands and expectations of literature. In practice, and most visibly, it is the Party which issues guidelines for the literary development, which outlines huge literary research programs, and which, through certain institutions and other channels, exerts a more or less tight control over the entire literary life of East Germany. Also, East German literary criticism applies the criteria of "Socialist Realism" in a rather rigid way, dismissing formal deficiencies as correctible imperfections, while attacking fiercely any evidence of "wrong consciousness." Publicity — and even criticism — of a work starts well in advance of publication; a writer is expected to listen to suggestions of the "Kollektiv" during the creative process of writing.

An example of the interaction of writer and society is the so-called "Bitterfeld Movement" launched in 1959. Goals of the movement were to bring writers into direct contact with the economic base, to bridge the gulf between life and art, and thereby to promote the kind of literature necessary on the now attained level on development of a socialist society. In practice, this campaign was designed to motivate writers to work at some place in the economic production on the basis of a contract, and the workers or farmers of the "Kollektiv" were encouraged to "pick up the pen" themselves.

Although the "Bitterfeld Movement" was an episode rather than a full success, it is typical enough of the official cultural politics followed in East Germany. Thus, it is understandable that many people in the western world are prepared to see in every work of art created in a socialist country a typical example of Socialist Realism. A typical example of Socialist Realism might be a painting or a statue of this kind: the muscular figure of a worker, lifting a red banner into the wind, his posture expressing revolutionary verve, his clenched fist showing determination, and the optimistic look on his face indicating his unshakeable belief in the final victory of the communist cause.

This is a caricature, and it is equally easy for a marxist to paint a repulsive picture of the average product of "decadent bourgeois mass culture." However, this much is true about the caricature or simplification of the "new hero" just outlined: the aesthetic theory of marxism-leninism requires indeed selection of representative subject matter, popularity ("Volksverbundenheit"), optimism, and, most of all, firm footing in the marxist doctrine ("Parteilichkeit").

Connected with this last point, but also inherent in the other principles, is what appears to be the crucial problem of Socialist Realism; to use a paradoxical formulation of it: because Socialist Realism is built on socialistic ideas, it has an antirealistic tendency in it. According to the theory of marxist-leninist aesthetics, a work of art may not be just any image of reality as reflected in the artist, but the true work of art is a carefully and consciously worked out model of "true reality," "truth" referring to the underlying social processes, which might be hidden under the surface appearance of history. Thus, a distinction is made between relevant and accidental facts — the latter may even be seriously misleading and therefore dangerous, in case they reflect historically obsolete attitudes. What is "real" in reality must be determined on the basis of the insights of the marxist classics, as interpreted by the Party. Consequently, "truth," "sincerity," and the like will mean different things for people with different beliefs; what a western liberal may call "telling the truth," striving for utmost objectivity, even against his personal biases, may mean, for a communist, to fall into the deviation of "objectivism," a deviation which is seen as characteristic of decadence.

One of the many thought patterns used to justify the distinction between representative and non-representative material is the "perspective of the future," as exemplified by Ulbricht in the above incident. Actually, anyone

3

who believes in some kind of development of history will select and interpret the raw material of his experience in the light of his or her basic beliefs. And even without such beliefs, a writer is subject to various kinds of influences which force him to write in one way rather than another. This is frequently overlooked by people who speak of the absolute autonomy and autarchy of the artistic realm. Whatever the full range of influences upon a writer, a western observer is prone to see, in the cultural life of the East European Communist countries, an intrusion of a political clique, and to speak of "cultural bolshevism." Now it is a fact that in the leninist continuation of marxism (and even more so in Stalin's theory and practice), the role of the Party is all-important. The Party is defined not only as the motor of political and economic development, but also as the "pacemaker" of the cultural development. Thus, Christa Wolf's novel *Der geteilte Himmel* was criticized, because she allegedly failed to show the "leading role of the Party."[2]

The perspective of the future, derived from firm footing in the marxist theory, entails optimism; that is, the East German author is expected to be optimistic about present and future developments. Since the revolution has successfully removed all basic alienation, any conflicts within a socialist society — and between socialist nations — can only be non-antagonistic conflicts, i.e. those conflicts are minor and in principle solvable. And since the road of socialism is basically correct, there is neither need nor even room for the bourgeois belief that doubts and scepticism are the motor of progress.[3]

As for the application of Socialist Realism by critics and politicians, there is the usual complex relationship between theory and practice. Since the medium of language is a rather abstract and intricate one in itself, the application of abstract aesthetic categories is likely to be complicated and even controversial. The category "Volksverbundenheit" (popularity), for example, can be used to justify crude naturalism, but it has also been used to attack mere documentary works. In the latter case, it would be called an insult to the people the author writes about, if he should just repeat for them what they already know and say; instead, he should, based on his close contact with those people and their Party, present a deeper analysis of their situation, show the real causes of their conflicts, connect their particular problems to the process of the entire society's development, and so on.

4

East German writers and critics know themselves how ill-defined many of the basic terms of Socialist Realism are. "Formalism" is one of the milder, yet definitely negative categories of official marxistic literary criticism. In marxistic philosophy, economic structures and property relationships are regarded as basic; the "superstructure" of culture built upon this base is held to be secondary to "content". In connection with this principle, "form" is regarded as secondary to "content" in literature. "Formalism," then, means undue emphasis on formal aspects, but more than anything else, it means the absence of required "positive" qualities in a work of art.

The attacks on Brecht's "Das Verhör des Lukullus" are perhaps the best-known examples of formalism charges.[4] In his feud with the famous marxist theoretician Georg Lukács, Brecht had charged Lukács himself with "formalistic elements" in his theory of realism.[5] The charge of formalism is often connected with the verdict of "decadence," as was the case in the just mentioned attacks on Brecht. It is interesting to note that Kant alludes to this literary quarrel by having a dogmatic teacher call Brecht's play "decadent."[6]

This leads us to another point: not only are central terms of Socialist Realism ill-defined, but their definitions change with the times. The episode just referred to in Kant's *Aula* concerning Brecht's play appears, in its context, to be a reminiscence of post-war times in East Germany, years which may be characterized on the basis as showing a German brand of stalinism. Since then, however, changes have taken place. These changes do not constitute smooth, continuous progress or liberalization in the Western sense. An example of the changes taking place in East Germany is that it is no longer officially believed that a writer takes over part of another writer's ideology just because he uses the other writer's techniques. Thus, techniques that had been banned as "formalistic" or "decadent," have by now become reputable; and there is hope — or at least the possibility of hope — for further evolution of the theory and practice of Socialist Realism. There exist, of course, sharply differing opinions as to how far socialist societies can be changed into more liberal systems. Only time will give a definite answer. But it should not be overlooked, in my opinion, that the communist ideology contains a strong humanistic heritage, completely absent from ideologies such as Hitler's fascism.

5

In a more thorough description of the literary scene in East Germany, one would have to name the various groups and traditions in East German literature; the older generation for example, which had been fighting for decades for a new society, is sharply distinguished from the younger generation which grew, as it were, into the established new society; and cross-cutting the generations, there are still old controversies surviving and being revived, such as that concerning the role of the arts in a socialist society, the role of non-socialist art, the role of the various literary and educational traditions, and so on.[7]

I have dwelt somewhat on various aspects of Socialist Realism and of the literary scene in East Germany because misjudgments are likely to occur if this background is ignored or neglected. For example, there is the wide-spread opinion that East German literature is backward, provincial, parochial; and, more gravely yet, one encounters charges of "dishonesty" and the like levelled against East German writers. There are certainly cynics and opportunists in every known society, and the socialist societies are no exception. However, if one is indeed to include considerations of an ethical nature in literary analysis, one should also feel the moral obligation to be as fair and objective as possible.

The West German critic Jörg Bernhard Bilke calls the *Aula* "basically dishonest" because, in his opinion, it keeps silent about too many events and facts, thus not overstepping the scope allowed by the Party ("Doch ist das Buch, weil es zu viel verschweigt [der 17. Juni fällt aus!] und somit innerhalb des von der SED zugestandenen Spielraums bleibt, im Grunde unaufrichtig.").[8] Obviously, Bilke has basic beliefs and political concepts rather different from Kant's, but I see no reason to doubt that Kant's beliefs are as well in accordance with his writings as is presumably the case with Bilke's beliefs and writings.

Furthermore, Kant does face up to many controversial events and facts in his society; and one should grant him the right to distinguish between the present reality of the Party on the one hand, and, on the other hand, what the Party as an ideal stands for. There are indications that Kant is painfully aware of unresolved problems, and even of embarrassing contradictions within himself and his society. Two brief examples to support this claim: first, the largely autobiographical hero of Kant's second novel *Das Impressum* uses several variations of the formula "That tears me apart!" over and over again; secondly — and similarly pointing to certain unresolved conflicts — the hero of the *Aula* is leitmotivically referred to as being an "Affe" (monkey or ape).

6

To be sure, awareness and criticism of stifling conditions are never expressed as bluntly or aggressively as in Biermann's works; but then, Biermann is an exceptional case, and Bilke himself does not extend the charge of "Unaufrichtigkeit" to Kunert's poems, which he describes as being parabolic and therefore multiply interpretable. Kant, with his indirect way of writing, indeed resembles authors like Kunert and Brecht; and one of the main goals of this book will be to investigate this element of indirectness as fully as possible.

Ironically enough, Kant is chastised for omitting the same important political events by East German critics as well — but for other reasons. The East German critics Silvia and Dieter Schlenstedt reproach Kant for not having made full use of the basic outline and possibilities of his main character, more specifically for omitting important events between 1949 and 1962.[9] This shows that refusing to comment on things may be in itself a message well understood by those living within the same system. Kant's refusal to comment on the events of June 17, 1953 — the famous strikes and uprisings of the East German populace against government and Party — and on the Berlin Wall are the more noticeable since both topics are mentioned in a travel scene (54 ff.). A close analysis of this scene will reveal that this is, if anything, an expressive silence ("beredtes Schweigen").[10] The official term „antifaschistischer Schutzwall" (anti-fascistic defense wall) is avoided throughout the *Aula*; instead, the word "Mauer" (wall) is used. Furthermore, Kant mentions and quotes from Heine's poem "Deutschland, ein Wintermärchen" (55), and, in connection with the West Berlin "Straße des 17. Juni," alludes to the short story "Die Kommandeuse" by Stefan Hermlin, a story which is rather controversial in the GDR (55).[11] Kant does deal with the topic of June 17th, 1953 in the *Impressum*, but that goes beyond the scope of this introduction.

The last sentence of the *Aula* reads "Hier ist niemand tot, und hier ist auch niemand zornig, und hier wird schon noch geredet werden" (464) (There is no one dead here, and there is no one enraged here, and there will be a speech here yet.). Kant alludes here to an autobiographical fact: in an interview, Kant said that he had started writing the *Aula* after he got very angry at a rather poor, dry description of the history of his school. At that point, he said, he decided that he could do a better job himself. Beyond this playful self-reference, Kant rejects in these lines the pose of the enraged accuser, but does not overlook

7

that some things are unfulfilled as of yet. Kant's hero Iswall expresses here his hope for a less restricted, less problematic time — after all, a dogmatic Party official, the Dean, withdrew his invitation for Iswall to give the closing speech when Iswall made it clear to him that he was not going to conform to the Dean's narrow and hollow categories. Thus, Kant seems to be suggesting that the entire book *is* the Aula speech. Times did change in East Germany, there was the process of de-stalinization, and Kant summarizes at the end of his book his position as that of conditional optimism. The reader will have to make up his own mind whether to call the *Aula* or its author dishonest after following the novel through.

The objection of parochialism, too, should be answered individually for each East German literary work. However, it may be worthwhile to consider the following more general argumentation: in a totalitarian society, there exists in principle, in contrast to a pluralistic society, a "correct" answer to every question, or it is believed that this ist the case; certain stereotypes, clichés, and conventions are not supposed to be questioned; in short, everything and everyone is from the beginning in a given frame of reference. Even if we take the terms "totalitarian" and "pluralistic" as relative, it is obvious that the "frame of reference" is narrower in the East German case than, for example, in the West German case. Thus, theoretical considerations as well as practical circumstances force a writer in the GDR to focus on the situation around him, including the selection of available literature from abroad. The result is indeed a relatively small range of themes in East German literature, usually traditional techniques, and frequent cross-references to other East German authors. It would be a wrong inference, however, to condemn this particular literary situation with a sweeping generalization such as "drab provincialism"; a discriminating evaluation would yield, among other results, that a text written in East Germany might be labeled allusive, implicit, and abbreviated; yet had the same text been written in West Germany, it would have perhaps been called cryptic — provided the reader could detect the allusions to begin with.

East German criticism of the *Aula* has generally been favorable, but almost exclusively on the grounds that the book constitutes a "Laudatio auf die DDR" (eulogy of the GDR), as the title of Kähler's article states programmatically.[12] On the other hand, whenever some critics saw difficult problems treated "improperly," such as the theme of escape from the GDR, they would speak of "schlimme Stellen" (objectionable passages).[13]

Also, Werner Neubert's paper "Komisches und Satirisches in Hermann Kants 'Aula' " (Comical and Satirical Elements in Hermann Kant's *Aula*) focuses on the content and especially on ideological questions, but does not include an analysis of Kant's satirical techniques; Neubert concentrates his main efforts on showing that although Kant criticizes small deficiencies in East German practices — deficiencies of the difficult post-war years — he does basically agree with the new socialist order.[14]

In their paper "Modern erzählt," the East German critics Silvia and Dieter Schlenstedt contribute valuable material for an analysis of certain structures in the *Aula*, but this paper, too, has the tendency of being apologetic rather than analytic.

Also in the contributions of Western scholars, formal aspects are not given enough attention. In his comparison of Christa Wolf's *Der Geteilte Himmel* and Kant's *Aula*, Hans-Georg Hölsken focuses on ideas of the Havemann circle and the Czechoslovakian reform communists, but fails to give a detailed and differentiated account of the literary techniques employed to convey these ideas. Similarly, Jost Hermand's brilliant chapter on the *Aula* in his book *Unbequeme Literatur* does not deal with formal considerations in detail.[15]

Satire, irony, and humor are generally recognized as important features of the *Aula*. These three qualities are ways of saying things indirectly; this means, they may be lost, if unrecognized; yet, if recognized, their functions are still open to interpretation. At worst, one does not see anything but a smooth surface: nice entertainment, interesting information, intelligent remarks — in one word, just "Socialist Biedermeier," but no high art. This is what I regard as the strongest, most serious objection to Kant's *Aula*; and these objections have indeed been raised by Raddatz in his knowledgeable and critical assessment of East German literature.[16] Raddatz fails to see "anything ambivalent, any hollow notes or half-steps" in the *Aula* ("Ambivalentes, Zwischen- oder Hohltöne").[17] He goes so far as to speak of "jongleurhafte Beliebigkeit" (jugglerlike arbitrariness).[18]

This brief survey of papers and book chapters written to date on Kant's *Aula* has shown that detailed studies both on form and content of the *Aula* are lacking. The study undertaken in this book tries to close this gap. This book comprises various methods, and even includes extra-literary material, where necessary, for understanding the *Aula*. The next chapter deals with the narrative point of view and the function of the focal character. From this I shall derive a basic category "dialectical humor" which will serve as a guideline, connecting the discussions of style, language, structure, and theme.

The establishing of dialectical humor as the basic principle of Kant's writing will refute Raddatz's negative criticism. I do admit, however, that the balance between "surface structure" and "deep structure" in Kant's art is a delicate one; Kant's second novel *Das Impressum* does not keep this balance as masterly as the *Aula* does.

I would like to conclude this introduction by giving a sample interpretation which both exemplifies the method used in this book to analyze the *Aula* and opens up new questions, as well. In Kant's *Aula*, the hero's inner monolog contains the following passage. When riding on an East German highway, the narrator sees a West German truck hauling cigarettes, which prompts, among others, the following thoughts within a long, inner monolog: "der Sattelschlepper ... fährt Zigaretten, dieser Provokateur fährt hundertzwanzig Kubikmeter HB durch die Deutsche Demokratische Republik, den hat das Lemmer-Ministerium angeworben, zwecks Erregung innerdeutschen Neides fährt der hier...."(461), ("that truck is hauling cigarettes; this provocateur hauls 120 cubic meters of HB through the German Democratic Republic; that State Secretary Lemmer hired him; to arouse intra-German envy, that's why he's driving here....").

East German cigarettes were — and still are — of low quality, whereas "HB" is the brand name of a West German, British-American Tobacco cigarette, then very popular. With this much information, we understand these lines as the playfully exaggerated fantasies of a passionate smoker named Iswall. But the passage implies much more than just exaggerated fantasies of a smoker. The word "innerdeutsch" (intra-German) alludes to the "Gesamtdeutsches Ministerium" — the West German State Department for East German affairs — which, by its very name, implies that only one German state exists and, therefore, that all relationships between East and West Germany can only be "innerdeutsch" (intra-German). The State Department is referred to here as the "Lemmer-Ministerium," a derogatery coinage of East German political language, polemically directed against Mr. Lemmer, the former head of that department. Thus one can see from these examples that this passage contains criticism of some aspects of West German politics and bureaucracy, most obviously contained in the mock bureaucratic phrase "zwecks Erregung innerdeutschen Neides" ("for the purpose of arousing intra-German envy"). Still more terms echo East German political propaganda — "Provokateur," "anwerben" (the opposite of "abwerben," the technical expression for inducing East German people to leave East Germany), and the emphatic use of "Deutsche Demokratische Republik." (The official West German language regulations required at that time to put the name "Deutsche Demokratische Republik" at least in quotation marks or to add "so-called" before the name, if one did not use the preferred West German term for East Germany, namely "Sowjetische Besatzungszone" or SBZ — the Soviet Occupation Zone.). However, there is clearly irony involved here; how serious, then, is this recital of propaganda? (I should add at this point in passing that terms like "Propaganda," "Agitation und Propaganda," etc. do not necessarily have the negative connotations these words have in English, or in the German spoken in Austria, Switzerland, or West Germany.). The question arises then as to who is really the "agent provocateur" since the West German "Gesamtdeutsches Ministerium" had obviously not hired the truck. The answer seems to be that in this case the alleged provocation must be blamed on East German politics and policies. The truck is perhaps coming from the Leipzig Fair, where prospective business partners are treated better than the average East German citizen (417). Or else, the truck may be supplying the "Intershops," which every East German reader knows about. In these shops, tourists from Western countries can buy liquor, cigarettes, etc. for less than it would cost them in their home countries, as long as they pay in foreign currency. The existence of these shops constantly reminds East German people that their hard-earned money still cannot compete with the hard currencies of Western countries — and this is indeed a source of resentment among the East German people. The "correct" answer to the question of "Intershops" is presumably that this is not a case of discrimination, but only a temporary measure, designed to exploit a weak spot in the exploitative capitalistic countries.

Intershops play only one small part in the problematic economic relationships between East and West Germany. Concerning the East German view of these economic relationships, this much has to be said: there was indeed some tendency in West Germany to boast about her economic superiority over East Germany; and the official East German opinion has it that West Germany tried to take advantage of the economic difficulties whenever possible, not refraining even from sabotage.

With this background information in mind then, one asks what does Kant really mean? Does he want to imply that such a minor problem as a shortage of good cigarettes should simply be laughed away if seen in proper perspective; or is he concealing behind this smoke-screen of a smoker's rambling fantasies a basic criticism of the East German system? Or does Kant take a position that lies beyond this alternative? To answer this question on the basis of a small, isolated text, would mean an over-interpretation; for a full interpretation one would have to discuss the function of other aspects of this text and its context, such as associative style, elements of colloquial language, the person sepaking (or thinking), and other occurrences of motives involved.

However, I trust I have made three points clear in interpreting this passage: first, to discuss the *Aula* — or any East German novel — it is necessary to be familiar with all relevant social conditions which determine the text and which the text in turn is aimed at; secondly, that close attention must be paid to the allusive and, at times, elusive forms of the text; and thirdly, that irony and humor seem to be important features of Hermann Kant's *Aula*.

"AFFE ISWALL" — THE CENTRAL CHARACTER AS SUBJECT AND OBJECT OF DIALECTICAL HUMOR

Narrative point of view

Despite some of their criticism, East German critics acknowledge and recognize that Robert Iswall is well-chosen for the central role in the *Aula*. However, the Schlenstedts go too far in equating Iswall with the author, and in calling Kant-Iswall a "general intellectual character" who represents mankind in a better and more real sense than bourgeois intellectuals could.[19]

Certainly, there are far-reaching parallels between Iswall's life and development and Kant's own biography; and Kant does use the figure Iswall to a certain extent as his mouth-piece, but the characteristics and functions of this central figure go well beyond simple representation of the author. In a panel discussion, Kant complained about he readers' fixation and preoccupation with autobiographical elements in his novel.[20] Therefore, taking his hint, I will not burden this book with biographical comparisons. It is my contention that the figure Iswall is a carefully chosen and worked out medium with specific advantages and intended limitations, and that a narrow focus on biographical details could obscure rather than illuminate Iswall's artistic functions.

Technically, the novel is written from a non-participant point of view; however, the perspective of the novel is entirely restricted to the perceptions and reflections of the central character Iswall. Thus, one might call Iswall the objectified narrator.

It is not certain on first sight in some cases who is actually speaking. In the opening scene, for example, the impression is first created that the author is describing a man writing a newspaper article, and that this man is perhaps the author himself; but gradually, it becomes apparent that this entire scene is a projected introspection by the character Iswall. Iswall is, so to speak, his own author, but prefers to talk about himself in the distant third person. This oscillation between subjective atmosphere and objective form reappears on different levels. Although the author never admits his presence, he succeeds, nevertheless, in creating the impression that he is always present.

This peculiar narrative point of view means that the distinction between "Reflexionsebene" (plane of reflection) and "Geschehnisebene" (plane of action), which the Schlenstedts emphasize as important, is actually only relative. Also the directly related events and even the dialogs are embedded in Iswall's attempt to remember and evaluate the past, and to connect it to the present. In the last analysis, narration, too, is Iswall's objectified reflection. This is not to say that the "reflection plane" is negligible; on the contrary, the openly reflective parts are essential for the full meaning of the novel. In the play which has been made out of the *Aula* by an East German adapter, most of these reflections have unfortunately been lost, and the character of Iswall has thus been markedly altered.

Iswall is not only the "central intelligence" of the novel, but he exemplifies, as a literary character, the achievements and dangers of his new socialist society. He is an example of the "new" equality, which makes it possible for him, an electrician, to go to college and become a journalist and free-lance writer; but, on the other hand, he is a member of the Communist Party, and, as such, he finds himself misusing his institutional power to betray his best friend.

The choice of making the central character a journalist and free-lance writer is fitting for several reasons, and an example of multifunctional motifs. For a journalist and writer, there is no sharp borderline between work and leisure, between job duties, social obligations, and purely private interests; the journalistic profession turns the vice of curiosity into a virtue, as Iswall puts it (408). Furthermore, journalistic work is socially relevant without being restricted to mechanical labor.

The intricate combination of contradictions and contrasts is one of the outstanding features of the entire *Aula*; I will first analyze contradictions and conflicts in the central character and then relate the results to style, structure, and contents of the novel.

The leitmotif "Affe Iswall"

The references to Iswall as an "Affe" (monkey or ape) constitute one of the leitmotifs of the book. This device draws attention to and ties together quite different aspects of Iswall's character.[21] Kant does not idealize his hero, but instead brings out several negative aspects of Iswall's character. The metaphor "Affe" suggests that Iswall is (at times at least, or in certain respects) a brute who has not yet finished the process of humanization. Similarly, when being overcome by jealousy, he turns again into a "Neandertaler" (455). These negative characteristics stand out even more, since Iswall shows otherwise and elsewhere the attributes of the socialist "new man."

The "Affe" motif is preluded by Iswall's inviting a girl to the circus mainly because "they have monkeys there." He gets her to agree that monkeys are funny and that she likes monkeys: "Die haben Affen da, und die finden Sie doch auch lustig, nicht? Oder mögen Sie keine Affen?" "Doch," sagte Inga, "Affen schon." (48 f.) ("They have monkeys there; and you find them funny, don't you? Or don't you like monkeys?" "Sure, I do," said Inga, "monkeys, I like.") Strangely enough, during their visit to the circus, monkeys are not even mentioned; on the other hand, however, Iswall makes fun of Inga's dress, thereby spoiling the mood, and Inga finally calls the whole circus "a silly thing." Are we to conclude that our expectation of hearing more of monkeys is ironically fulfilled by Iswall behaving like a monkey himself, by his being the "Hauptaffe" (most apelike) in this scene?[22] At any rate, it is significant that Iswall's future nickname "Affe" is foreshodawed by his regarding monkeys as the main attraction of the circus. At the same time, the scene makes the reader aware of the possible negative consequences of Iswall's habit of joking.

Insecurity as the source of Iswall's "Affigkeit" (monkeyism or aphishness)

There are two types of situations in which Iswall displays the negative sides of being a monkey or ape: either he feels overly elated about a success (even if it is only the success of a joke), or he feels unable to cope with a situation. The common element in both cases is inner insecurity.[23] In one such scene, his friend "scientifically unmasks" him, suggesting that Iswall behaves like this for certain psychological reasons (166 f.).

In particular where his relationship to a girl is involved, Iswall lacks self-confidence and trust. It is this insecurity that causes him to hurt his first girl-friend at the beginning of their relationship with the remark about her dress (49); for the same reason, he insults Miss Schmöde, since

15

he is in that situation too strongly reminded of unresolved problems in his relationship with his girl-friend (165 ff.); and this inner insecurity is the ultimate reason for his betraying his best friend (408).

The conclusion that concealed under Iswall's jokes there is insecurity and sensitivity is supported by the observation that Iswall shrinks back from using big words like "love"; and as for talk about sexual matters, he or his friends will go only as far as to speak of "touching a girl's knee and all that stuff" (126).

The *Aula* offers several explanations and motivations for Iswall's monkey-like qualities; Iswall himself blames the acquisition of his "big mouth" on his having been in a prison camp (49). There is also a sociological explanation for Iswall's joking: his comrade Filter knows that city people are likely to poke fun at other people (71).

There are deeper reasons for Iswall's behavior than those given in his humorous understatements. Iswall's psychic development is marked by stress and great shifts: he loses his father early; he has to live through the horrors of war; he experiences life in a prison camp as a young man; he is "re-educated" in an anti-fascistic institute connected with the prison camp; and later on he is faced with various difficulties connected with advancement in his new socialist society. A psychologist may see here only acculturation and socialization conflicts, and speak of the typical inferiority complex and the resulting over-compensation. Kant, however, does not elaborate on any psychological explanations, but presents only reactions to Iswall's behavior and reflections by Iswall himself. Thus, Iswall undertakes his own layman's analysis, which may indeed be a parody on the psychoanalytic or some other psychological theory. In his self-analysis, Iswall sees himself split into two opposing persons, an "Außen-Iswall," and an "Innen-Iswall" (411). The first term, the "outer Iswall," refers to the role he is assuming for other people, because the feelings of the "inner Iswall" are dangerously vulnerable and difficult to control. This role, or masque, of a clown, a jokester, a "monkey," easily gives the impression of a boastful, arrogant, and conceited person, for example "der Angeber Iswall," (320), "Hochmut," (303), etc.[24]

Iswall carries his self-analysis further: he speaks of his tendency to swallow protest and behave ("Bereitschaft, Widerspruch zu verschlucken und brav zu sein," 171); or he calls himself silly and a romantic, remembering his sentimental feelings when returning home from the prison camp ("Gleichzeitig lachte er sich aus, und er nannte sich einen

Romantiker, und er erkannte den albernen Jüngling . . ." 269). The critical remarks about himself are again usually multifunctional, as will be demonstrated in the next section.

Imitation as ironic compliance

The most obvious element of Iswall's monkeyism is imitation, as manifest in the following two scenes. When asked by his step-father to act the role of a reactionary peasant, he does so well that the step-father cannot convince him of the advantages of socialist farming (124). Iswall's talent for imitation and parody, together with his intellectuality, wit, and imagination, make him a good entertainer and allow him to master difficult situations. He demonstrates his talent of witty retorts in many well-told stories and anecdotes within the *Aula*, as well as in every-day conversations. When someone calls Iswall early in the morning and politely asks, "Did I call too early," Iswall replies: "That depends on what you want of me . . . if it is a speech, you are too late. For speeches, a half year's notice is required." ("Das hängt davon ab, was Sie von mir wollen . . . wenn es eine Rede ist, dann ist es zu spät. Für Reden gilt eine Meldefrist von einem halben Jahr," 33). The unexpected beginning "That depends" is resolved in the humorous conversion of „too early" into "too late," where Iswall playfully pretends to take his partner's polite formula literally. The "requirement of a half year's notice for a speech" alludes to the Aula speech Iswall has just been requested to prepare and is directed more to the reader than to the telephone caller. Using bureaucratic language parodistically gives the anticipated refusal an acceptable tone.

In a scene with his former dean, Iswall uses the technique of imitation in an ironic way as a means of self-defense. His answer "völlig richtig" (exactly right) to an imposing suggestion of his partner is actually a quotation; he imitates his partner who has already used this expression several times (267). It adds to the flavor of the scene when the other person, a bureaucratic Party official, takes this only as compliance and does not notice the implied refusal. Iswall's "Völlig richtig!" is not a complete refusal either; he agrees with the idea of the suggestion, namely to show how his former classmates of the Workers' and Peasants' College are now holding responsible positions, but he rejects the cliché rhetoric

17

and the shallow optimism of this functionary; and he resents the censorship which is veiled in the studied casualness of advice and suggestions.

In both scenes mentioned above, the real addressee of Iswall's irony is obviously the reader. In the fictive situation, however, Iswall is both an actor and his own audience. Imitation in the above scenes is best described as ironic compliance: when faced with an obstacle he cannot overcome objectively, he pretends to comply outwardly, yet inwardly he maintains his independence.

Iswall is aware of his shortcomings and of his playing the role of a "monkey," and he makes this very awareness the object of his monkey-like jokes. Typical is the following small episode. Iswall used to make the following comment at least once a week about the depressing look of the eye-clinic in which his wife works: "But that doesn't matter anyway, since all your customers have bad eyes!" ("Aber das tut ja nichts," sagte Robert mindestens einmal in der Woche, "wo eure Kunden ja doch alle einen Augenschaden haben!" 25). In an ironic attempt at self-criticism, Iswall decides that in the future he will tell his joke *less* than once a week. Similarly, the repeated mentioning of his excessive smoking is an admission of a bad habit and, at the same time, a practice field for his humor (7, 22, 231, 243); one feels strongly reminded of Wilhelm Busch's analysis of self-criticism in the poem by the same name, "Die Selbstkritik."

Iswall's humor does seem a bit strained in the railway scene (61): his verbosity is not quite plausible in the situation, and the excessive use of assonances is rather manneristic ("d wie Dogma, Dom, Diözese, Diakon oder Drommete" 61, "b wie Bischof, Bibel, Bethlehem oder Bannbulle" 62). Nevertheless, Iswall's speech is motivated by the situation: a boisterous upstart from West Germany had gotten on his nerves just before, so his speech is some kind of humorous off-reaction through imitation, and, at the same time, it is a satire on conservative and clerical features in West Germany. Beyond that, the mannerism of alliteration may be a satirical reference to contemporary West German authors like Grass.

"Monkeyism" as a masque of the moralist Iswall

Iswall does not solve problems objectively by "playing a monkey," but he does master problems subjectively, yielding to his inner urge to name and re-name things. He admits that he likes to talk (448), and he subscribes to the principle "Was nicht buchstabiert wird, ist nicht" — "What isn't spelled out, doesn't exist" (452). However, there is more involved than just some defense mechanism: Iswall's self-stylization as a "monkey" is largely ironical — the mimicry of a moralist who tries to preach in an indirect and thereby more humane way than he would otherwise; and it is a play featuring himself as the scapegoat of his society. We see here the old technique of telling the truth laughingly, the difference being that Kant-Iswall does not presume to know the whole truth.

The motif of using "negative" means for a "positive" end reoccurs in other works by Kant. In his short-story "Die Werbung," the hero resorts to pretending intellectual arrogance in order to lure a gifted printer back to school so that the young printer can get a college education.[25] Also in Kant's second novel, *Das Impressum*, there is repeated reference to a "positive scheming" initiated by the central character to help people master their lives.

Iswall makes the moral impetus in him for teaching and helping others the object of this humor. He refers to himself as "Sittenrichter Iswall" (Morals Judge, Iswall, 422) and "Moraltute Iswall" (Morals Trumpet, Iswall, 240), and he falls into sermonistic and prayer-like style several times, as in "Stehe auf und renne.... Amen" ("Rise up and run.... Amen", 128).[26]

There is also self-irony involved when he gives a summary of his life in religious terms and in a style which reminds one strongly of Luther's biblical language: Iswall mentions his own conversion to communism after a symbolical death, and then the ensuing command given to him to save other people in the name of communism (410).

When his first girlfriend (incidentally, the daughter of a minister) detects the "preacher-tone" in Iswall's speech, the form of Iswall's speech is ridiculed as is any pseudo-religious facade that might obstruct the rational and scientific nature of marxism; but it is, nevertheless, clear from other evidence that Iswall has deep socialist convictions (106). It is Iswall's insight that Inga would not change over to his cause nor even respect his position that finally breaks up their relationship.

19

Self-correction as a consequence of Iswall's being aware of his monkeyism

Self-criticism by Iswall concerning his exaggeration, his preacher's style, etc., may be implied or suggested; but frequently, Kant makes Iswall correct himself explicitly. In these cases, Kant allows himself to pursue direct satire up to a certain point, but then takes it back and invites the reader to make up his own mind about the problem. Iswall will call an idea he has pursued "nonsense" (13, 23 f., 406) or criticize it as inadequate, unjust, or silly (11, 275, 393, 403); but regardless, the "thesis" is still in the book and thereby preserved, however seriously Iswall afterwards revokes the thesis, and whatever the final synthesis. In this phenomenon, we note the importance of the "Affe-Iswall" motif for the structure of the *Aula* itself.

In the following example, Kant uses the technique of Iswall's self-correction to satirize the eulogists of "the good old days":

er selbst konnte diese Reden "Als wir noch in Holzpantoffeln herumliefen" nicht hören. Es war immer, als ob sich einer brüstete, er mache nun schon lange nicht mehr in die Hosen, aber schön, schön sei es gewesen, damals, als er es getan, schön und schwer, und vor allem letzteres sollten die nicht vergessen, die heutzutage dank der Anstrengungen ihrer Vorgänger gleichsam stubenrein auf die Welt kämen. Reden dieser Art waren Alterserscheinungen, persönliche oder die von Generationen, und Ansporn gaben sie nicht. Dieses Urteil war ungerecht, Robert spürte es; (10).

he himself could not listen to this kind of talk anymore — talk like: "When we were barefoot." It was always as if someone were boasting that he hadn't messed in his pants for the longest now; but it certainly had been beautiful, yes, beautiful, in those days when he did, beautiful and difficult, and especially this latter should never be forgotten by those who, these days, due to the efforts of their predecessors, entered the world weened, as it were. Talk of this kind was a phenomenon of aging, personal aging, or the aging of generations, and could not give any inspiration. This opinion was unjust, Robert felt it; (10).

The comparing of East German pioneers with babies still messing in their pants is grossly inadequate and contrasts comically with the high style in which this comparison is made. It is again typical of Iswall's inclination towards exaggeration, imitation, and repetition that the equation of the post-war generation with a messing baby is extended into some detail, using effectively convocation style. Iswall's self-correction leads him to the serious insight that one cannot have a future without a past (a thought also expressed in the Heine quote preceding the book); but the problem of dealing with the past, especially with its glamorous points, turns again into a train of thought which Iswall has to correct as "reeking of boastfulness" (11).

We might say that Kant, in these self-corrections, takes advantage of Iswall's fool's freedom. He includes a pun about Germany's special way to communism, a political theory banned officially in 1949:

"Wir haben übrigens noch mehr Räte. Aktivist Blank ist was Dickes im Volkswirtschaftsrat, Irmchen Strauch ist auch Studienrat, und Jakob Filter ist, glaube ich, Forstrat oder so etwas. Ist dies nun der besondere deutsche Weg zur Räterepublik?"
"Fauler Witz," sagte Riebenlamm, "von der Gewohnheit kommst du wohl auch nicht mehr los." (299 f.)

"By the way, we have still more 'Räte.' Activist Blank is a big shot in the 'Volkswirtschaftsrat' (State Economic Council), Little Irma Strauch ist 'Studienrat,' too, and Jakob Filter is, I believe, 'Forstrat' or something like that. Now, is this the special road Germany took to become 'Räterepublik'?" (299 f.)

(The above pun is based upon the two meanings of *Rat*. *Rat* is the traditional title for professional German state officials, as well as the name of a "council," in particular the name of a revolutionary "soviet" — which is to say that the term *Rat* is also the name of a committee representing a group of soldiers, farmers, workers, etc., elected by and from their respective group for a limited term.)

Iswall's partner calls the above a sick joke and intimates that Iswall will probably never get rid of the habit — but the joke itself with all its implications remains in the book. There are at least two things implied by the joke: first, a criticism of the fact that East Germany did not create its own brand of communism, but, while under Soviet occupation, copied instead the Russian model; and, secondly, a criticism of the fact that in East Germany's socialism, there are negative features of "Prussianism" still surviving, an implication also pointed out by Jost Hermand.[27]

The *Aula* closes with self-correction by the hero, and in this case, the antithesis definitely bears the stronger weight. The rejection of self-pity and the disclaiming of anger culminate in the promise that "there will be a speech here yet," with all that this implies.

These self-corrections, as I like to call Iswall's critical dialogs with himself, fulfill formally the famous practice of critique and self-critique; their function, however, is rather to criticize the common use of this principle. Marx had already written about the importance of self-criticism in a revolutionary party, and Lenin and Stalin emphasized this point strongly. In practice, however, this principle was perverted by Stalin long before the excesses of the great purges, with the ritualistic confessions of the accused; he used the watchwords "critique and self-critique" from 1925 on as an instrument of keeping in power and strengthening his political position. Several episodes in the *Aula* criticize the stalinistic ritual of critique and self-critique, usually by ridiculing it. Thus, Iswall is criticized on his first day on campus for causing delay and receives a hilarious lesson in the art of critique and self-critique — an art which he, in his own way, later develops to perfection (35 f.). In one of his reflections, Iswall ponders about the significance of the change from "critique and self-critique" to "struggle of opinions," which denotes a milder form of disagreement: "Wenn er sich nicht irrte, hatte das Wort zumindest im Bereich der Wissenschaft und Kunst den Doppelbegriff Kritik und Selbstkritik abgelöst und beschrieb eine mildere Variante der Auseinandersetzung" (35).

Thus, Iswall's self-corrections use the mechanics of critique and self-critique, while criticizing the mechanical ritual of critique and self-critique.

Dialectical humor as the source of dialogic structure

Iswall's self-corrections are also a means of evoking an atmosphere of dialog between Kant-Iswall and the reader. This element of dialog is reinforced by questions Iswall asks or is asked. It is easy for the reader to participate in this question process, since it is not always made clear as to who is asking the question or who is supposed to be answering the question.

In reflecting on a student demonstration, Iswall imagines a critical question, and in the imagined dialog playfully provokes the fictive, narrow-minded questioner into a misunderstanding:

Will dieser Herr Iswall etwa andeuten, es könne einen Gegensatz gegeben haben zwischen dem, was die jungen Demonstranten auf dem Pommernplatz sagten und sangen, und dem, was sie dachten? Nein, das will Robert Iswall nicht sagen, obwohl sich natürlich Fälle denken ließen... Nur keine Aufregung; er wird das erläutern. (292)

Should this Mr. Iswall really be suggesting that there could have been a discrepancy between what those young demonstrators at the Pomerania Place said and sang, and what they thought? No, Robert Iswall does not mean to say that, although, of course, one could think of cases... Just don't get excited, please; he'll explain. (292)

In the formulation of the following question, which anticipates deviation ("Abweichung"), Iswall alludes to a scene which happened on his first day on campus: at that time, the stalinist teacher Angelhoff criticized the chairman of a meeting completely unnecessarily: "Sollen wir Ihren Worten, Kollege Völschow, entnehmen, daß sich eine Situation denken ließe, in der es nicht so wäre, wie Genosse Stalin sagt?" (30) ("Are we to gather from your words, Colleague Völschow, that a situation is conceivable in which it would not be as Comrade Stalin says?" 30).

In both of the above cases, Kant satirizes narrow-minded "proletarian watchfulness" — a traditional communist watchword given out during the post-war years, when the latter episode took place.

Throughout the *Aula* there are satirical references to the ritualistic, stereotyped, rhetorical questions of narrow-minded, suspicious Party officials, for example the parody of the formulas "So kann man die Frage nicht stellen" (22), and "Und was ist die Folge? Dies ist die Folge:..." (160). These rhetorical questions are also a favorite target of the existing East German satirical cabarets. Kant's criticism goes further than just to ridicule the poor speech habits of many Party officials; Kant seems to satirize the underlying principle of admitting only those questions for which there are known answers.

As opposed to the hollow, rhetorical questions just mentioned and in contrast to their open or disguised dogmatic answers, Kant-Iswall rarely, if ever, gives a simple answer to a question that might arise in the reader's mind. Rather, one gets the impression that the narrator uses the buddy-relationship established through a humorous caricature of himself to help the reader raise his own questions and to evaluate the various answers possible for him. And these constant ironies, paradoxes, and ambiguities amount to quite a few question marks.

When trying to remember what exactly he had said and thought on an important occasion, Iswall realizes that he knows little about himself and much less about other people — a variation of the Socratian saying "I know that I don't know." He concludes this section with the unusually serious "Ich weiß nur, daß ich fragen muß, wenn ich leben will — so viel habe ich immerhin mitbekommen bei Riebenlamm und Wanda und Haiduck und Danuta und einigen anderen," (439 f.). "I only know that I must question, if I am to live — I have at least gotten that much from Riebenlamm and Wanda and Haiduck and a few others," (439 f.). Here, I venture to say that Kant himself is speaking of the existential necessity to raise questions.

At this point the playful distance that Iswall has kept for himself through using the third person is overcome, and Iswall answers a question (raised by himself) in the first person. As in a film close-up, Iswall finally confesses to himself that he has failed in a certain situation (418–440).

Besides questions, there are other means that contribute to creating an atmosphere of dialog. Several times, Iswall calls explicitly upon the reader's experience in the face of something both know only too well. Thus, Iswall says in the long inner monolog concerning a demonstration that if one were to make a movie about this scene, no red color would be needed to bring out the red of the posters: "es [das Publikum] kennt doch das Leben, und es kennt auch eure Filme" (289) ("the public knows life after all, and it knows your films, too," 289.).[28]

At other places, as mentioned above, Kant has Iswall act in such a way that only the reader fully understands what is implied; Iswall's partner in the narrative situation does not understand. Thus the reader is given the feeling of knowing more than the persons in the novel.

We might say that Kant by-passes his characters and establishes between Iswall and the reader a close relationship of smiles and knowing winks.

Connected with what I call "dialogic atmosphere" is "dramatic flair." Kant shows a preference for theatrical settings in his scenes and episodes. If the reader is not called upon to be partner to a dialog, at least he is invited to feel like a spectator. Many scenes have a protagonist and an "audience," Iswall frequently taking the main protagonist's part. Even as an actor, Iswall's attitude is reflected to such an extent that he plays simultaneously the role of chorus and audience. Underneath, one can detect a fascination with dramatic conflicts and contradictions in life; Iswall relishes the following scene: he, a member of the East German Communist Party (SED), is lying on the couch of his West German brother-in-law, the "gangster," and overhears the words of a prostitute proposing to a tired longshoreman returning from work: "I am better than Cleopatra!" — and the retort, "And I bet a bit older, too!" (115).

The prevalent reflectiveness is somewhat symptomatic of the psychological state prevalent in East Germany. Looking at it from a positive point of view, one can say that the people of East Germany have generally more "consciousness" and more awareness of themselves and of political questions than the average West German does.[29] Most East German refugees, for instance, say that West Germans are dull compared to the East Germans, and that they miss the heightened awareness they had enjoyed in East Germany.[30] On the other hand, this higher awareness is an expression of a constant watchfulness as to what, in a certain situation, can be safely said, or what has to be said; in this sense, "quotation" is saying what one is supposed to say, but, at the same time, indicating by certain signals of irony that this is only a quote.

This reflectiveness or role playing can go too far; and critics of communism will be eager to speak of general hypocrisy, mass psychosis, or national schizophrenia. To generalize in this way is obviously an unjust description; and yet, this heightened awareness is a problem — perhaps the major problem for many people in East Germany. It is no coincidence, I feel, that Christa Wolf shows the sensitive main character of her novel *Nachdenken über Christa T.* suffering painfully from the role playing around her, mostly from the hypocrisy of her high-school students, a hypocrisy moreover which is equally hypocritically accepted, if not expected, by most of the teachers.[31]

Is the "Affe" motif expression of alienation?

The episode in which Iswall receives the nickname "Affe" is characterized by a combination of positive and negative results. A student demonstration for renaming the "Pommernplatz" is taking place, and, elated by what they regard as "revolutionary doings," the students — including Iswall — fail to protect one of their classmates from the vicious attacks and threats of a stalinist teacher — the result being that this gifted student flees to the West. When Party Secretary Haiduck, one of the idealized characters, learns of what happened, he gives Iswall a piece of his mind, culminating in the repeated words: "Iswall, du bist ein Affe!" (303), "Iswall, you are an ape!"

What is implied by this rebuke, and by the "Affe" leitmotif in general? The word itself has negative connotations, especially in the context of marxistic evolutionary (or revolutionary) theory. A basic thought in Marx's writings is the evolution and emancipation of man from the animal kingdom; Marx used the animal stage metaphorically and spoke of "Menschwerdung des Affen," referring to the process of humanization of the "Unmensch," that is, the humanization of someone who is dehumanized by being the object or subject of economic exploitation.[32] Engels even speaks in the title of a sketch written in 1876 of the "role of work in the process of the humanization of the ape" ("Über die Rolle der Arbeit im Prozeß der Vermenschlichung des Affen"). Nietzsche's comparison of ape, man, and superman in the prologue of his *Zarathustra* is even better known:

Ich lehre euch den Übermenschen. Der Mensch ist etwas, das überwunden werden soll. Was habt ihr getan, ihn zu überwinden?

Alle Wesen bisher schufen etwas über sich hinaus: und ihr wollt die Ebbe dieser großen Flut sein und lieber noch zum Tiere zurückgehen, als den Menschen überwinden?

Was ist der Affe für den Menschen? Ein Gelächter oder eine schmerzliche Scham. Und eben das soll der Mensch für den Übermenschen sein: ein Gelächter oder eine schmerzliche Scham.

Ihr habt den Weg vom Wurme zum Menschen gemacht, und vieles ist in euch noch Wurm. Einst wart ihr Affen, und auch jetzt noch ist der Mensch mehr Affe, als irgend ein Affe.

It teach you the Superman. Man is something that is to be surpassed. What have ye done to surpass man?

All beings hitherto have created something beyond themselves: and ye want to be the ebb of that great tide, and would rather go back to the beast than surpass man?

What is the ape to man? A laughing-stock, a thing of shame. And just the same shall man be to the Superman: a laughing-stock, a thing of shame.

Ye have made your way from the worm to man, and much within you is still worm. Once were ye apes, and even yet man is more of an ape than any of the apes.[33]

Does Kant suggest that Iswall is a brute who has not yet finished the process of humanization? How does he view the dialectics of the old and the new? Could he be implying that there is still alienation present in his society, even in its most progressive members? The question of alienation in a socialist society is a delicate one; it was heatedly discussed at the marxist Kafka Conference in Prague in 1963, with no unanimous answer being reached.

What is at issue here, beyond the controversy about a multifaceted philosophical term, is the very practical political question of whether the existing socialist societies have lived up to their promises yet, or whether major changes are still necessary.

The renowned Polish marxist Adam Schaff discusses the problem of "alienation" in socialism extensively in his book *Marxismus und Individuum*, where he also refers to the Prague Conference of 1963.[34] He says that although the Kafka discussion was officially about literature, it was actually marxists talking about their own socialist societies, namely about whether alienation still exists in them at present. The orthodox dogmatics produced evidence from Marx's writings where Marx expressed the belief that with the positive removal of private property, all resulting alienation would positively be removed.[35] On the other hand, many contended that in the intermediate stage of socialism, alienation might be present in many forms. Schaff mentions state, bureaucracy, army, family, work, nationalism, and privileged groups of people as areas of alienation. Schaff passionately pleads for recognizing these areas of alienation, lest they poison the atmosphere; at the same time, he realizes that almost nothing has been done thus far in the way of the immense scientific task this entails. His basic argument then is that there will be deep conflicts even in a socialist society, but that one has to acknowledge these conflicts. Curtailing the absolute freedom of artistic expression and of information may be necessary in periods of transition for political reasons, but it should be kept to an absolute minimum; sometimes one should run the risk of even admitting for example that different schools of marxism exist within the marxist countries; and any curtailing of freedom should always be officially admitted as an evil.

In my opinion, Kant implies the question of alienation, but does not give a clear answer to it himself. Kant does criticize misuse of Party power, he warns against the dangers of bureaucratism, he implies that the irrational sides of man should not be underestimated (Iswall happens to fall in love during the demonstration just mentioned above, and this distracts him more than anything else from paying attention to the plight of his classmate); however, rather than just illustrating abstract philosophical or political problems that have their solutions built-in by definition, Kant confronts himself and his readers with stories and metaphors reflecting the paradoxes of concrete experience.

As a marxist, Kant has deep roots in the enlightenment, its rationality, its didactic use of paradoxes, and its belief in progress. Lessing had animals speak and act like humans in his fables in order to bring out some truth more effectively and pleasantly; for a similar reason, Kant plays with the colloquial idiom "Du bist ein Affe!" (303, 412). Kant's humor is accompanied by optimism, but a critical and self-critical optimism, not to be mistaken for the shallow optimism derived mechanically from theory. Kant believes in enlightenment, that is, in the necessity and possibility of improving the world; and if his socialist society constitutes institutionalized enlightenment, Kant points out, with his dialectical humor, that real enlightenment can only be a permanent, self-critical process. The leitmotif complex "Affe Iswall" is, in this sense, an element of structural self-criticism.

28

A last example of dialectical humor may exemplify my point and conclude this chapter. A conversation between Iswall and his most respected teacher, during which they touch upon many issues, contains this passage: "Iswall, du bist ein Affe." "Ist das deine Meinung oder zitierst du?" "Beides. [...]" ("Iswall, you are a monkey." — "Is that your opinion, or are you quoting?" — "Both. [...]" 300). Iswall receives a paradoxical, unexpected answer instead of a clear-cut yes or no. He, and the reader with him, have to find their own answer — if the joke was meant to be more than just a joke.

DIALECTICAL HUMOR IN LANGUAGE, STYLE, AND STRUCTURE

Creative imitation and humorous contrast

Thus far I have tried to show how the leitmotif "Affe Iswall" represents conflicts of the central character, and how Kant uses his character's "monkeyism" to create a narrative framework in which playfulness and seriousness are closely interwoven. I call the use of the leitmotif "Affe Iswall" a prime example of "dialectical humor" — a term which encompasses a wide range of ironic, humorous, and comic techniques, all of which are multifunctional, combining assertion and negation, seriousness and playfulness. From here I will go on to show that dialectical humor is the organizing principle of style, language, and structure in the *Aula*. It may be argued, however, that the term *humor* itself contains an element of dialectics within it — which is true; but in the case of Kant, adding the term *dialectical* to the word *humor* underlines the dialectic finesse with which Kant treats elements of marxistic dialectics themselves.

In the following interpretation of the *Aula*'s language, style, and structure, I do not aim at an exhaustive analysis, nor do I use statistical methods. Furthermore, I do not separate the description of stylistic phenomena from the discussion of their function since I regard form and content as inseparable. To say that form and content are inseparable usually means that there is a given content for which the author has chosen a certain form; and usually it is seen as the task of the interpretation to prove that chosen form and underlying content are in harmony with each other, or in intentional disagreement, as the case may be. In the case of the *Aula*, however, one would miss the decisive point if one were to assume a content existing independently of form and structure: that is, I believe form and structure have meaning in themselves, and thus contribute actively to the content.

On the stylistic level, dialectical humor is characterized by creative imitation and humorous contrast. By creative imitation, I mean the techniques of quotation, allusion, parody, play on words, exaggeration, understatement, and paradox. These two terms are not mutually exclusive sub-categories of dialectical humor, but rather two fundamental aspects of Kant's style that lend themselves to the grouping of outstanding stylistic features.

Creation of new words

Kant's style is characterized by the creation of new words, the re-literalization of idioms, the individualistic re-definition of existing language, and by parodistic characterization.

New words are always formed in analogy to existing word formations by derivation, substitution, or composition. The following catalog of names of an imaginary profession combines the figure of variation with word creation. The newly formed words are by no means esoteric, but immediately understandable satires in extreme condensation. We find seven variations on the name of an imagined scentmixer's job for films of the future (286 ff.). The first form is an Anglo-German hybrid, a combination of the archaic word *Ruch* (smell) and *Mixer. Ruchmixer* — a satiric slant directed against the international garble of film makers. *Freund Nasenbetreuer* (Friend Nose-custodian) is a take-off on the bureaucratic euphemism *betreuen* (to take care of) and the official Party youth organization address *Jugendfreund* (youth-friend, brother, etc.) and similar forms. *Riechstoffmischer* (Smelling-substance-mixer) is the most objective, scientific expression, but the following "verehrter Kollege Gerucher oder wie du auch geheißen werden magst" ("respected Colleague Smeller or however you may be called") parodies again official nomenclature, as do the remaining phrases: "geplagter Vertreter der Abteilung Nase im Ton- und Lichtspielwesen" ("plagued representative of the section Nose, in the Department of Sight-and-Sound-Affairs"), *Filmbedufter* (Film-scenter), another variant of euphemistic professional names, and *Kollege Riecheur* (Colleague Smellerateur), the latter probably mocking a snobbish preference for the elegant flair of French derivations.

Most new word formations in the *Aula* are compounds of -*mensch*. A good example is found in the words of a reactionary mathematics teacher: "Als Mensch darf der Wissenschaftler selbstverständlich kein Unmensch sein. Aber als Wissenschaftler muß er sozusagen ein Nichtmensch sein. Ende der Debatte" (327). ("As a *human* a scientist must not be *inhuman*

31

of course. But as a scientist, he must so to speak be *non-human*. End of debate.")[36] This scene is a language caricature of what Kant sees as a schizophrenic, illogical belief in research for research's sake ("wertfreie Forschung"); the problem of amorality and immorality is neither objectified nor solved here, but rather humorously crystallized.

In the above case, language imitates attitudes. In a way, the technique used is imitative itself, since there are already established compounds with *-mensch* such as *Unmensch* (inhuman), *Übermensch* (superman), *Untermensch* (subhuman), or the colloquial *Zeitungsmensch* (newspaperman); what in language has long been recognized and called analogical extension, is used by Kant in a uniquely artistic way.

In the language of Grieper, Iswall's brother-in-law on the Hamburg Reeperbahn, we find excessive use of these' formations: *Schriftmensch*, *Kopfmensch*, *Fleißmensch*, *Kartenmensch* (153 ff.), *Polizeimensch* (220), *Wissensmensch* (221), *Denkmensch, Mitdenkmensch, Prahlmensch* (222), *Pfuschmensch* (223). Although humorously used, these words expose Grieper's basically inhuman attitude towards his fellow man: for him, people are reduced to functions and categories. In particular, his statement that woman is no "Denkmensch" (thinking-being) reveals the traditional opinion that women are basically irrational — perhaps another example of prejudices Kant finds in West German society. Kant lets Iswall continue the series of *-mensch* compounds in his usual "apish" way with *Verkaufsmensch* (225), *Wachmensch*, and *Schlafmensch* (231); and later with *Fleißmensch* (359).

Some further examples of analogous word formation: the term *Vorwärtsler* is contrasted satirically with the new formation *Rückwärtsler* (459, 462); we find *Kopfwerker* together with *Handwerker* (322), and *Nahstudium* (instead of the established *Direktstudium*) in the combination *Fern- und Nahstudium*, where Kant makes, at the same time, use of the fixed phrase *nah und fern* or even *Nah- und Fernverkehr* (407).

Re-definitions and re-literalizations

Kant likes to re-literalize expressions, to contrast the literal, concrete meaning of an idiom with its conventional, metaphorical meaning. Thus, the idiom "mitten ins Blaue" (at random, or haphazardly) is applied to a fictive machine's hand moving into the blue area of a gauge, which, in context, is a satirical taunt against narrow-minded Socialist Realism (14). A typical term in administrative language, *ungeklärte Angelegenheit* (an unclear matter), is made to refer to the reeking "Stadtgraben" (city mote, 288). A last example, the skiing term *Schußfahrt* (the descent of a skier) is understood literally as "shot-ride," evoking associations with other meanings of *shot* (403).

An even more important instance of Kant's re-evaluation of language is his rather subjective re-definition of existing words. For example, Kant uses *Brause* (soda-pop) to mean "casual love" (417). This equation was generalized from Iswall's personal experience, and, in a similar way, *Sonnenweg*, the street where he challenges his physically stronger enemy, becomes his personal word for the courage to face unsolved problems of the past (407). The field of Iswall's subjective experience is widened to include words and entire phrases which grow out of the friendship between Iswall and his roommates, and thus these words and phrases receive new definitions. To this category belong *Pappnase* and the question "Verstehst du das?"[37]

Translation into language

In all of the above cases we might speak of "translation into language"; a certain problem, a problematic attitude, a conflict or whatever it may be, is "translated" into a fitting language expression. There are other modes of expressing reality in language besides translation into language, such as symbolization and description. Indeed Kant does employ these modes, but the imitative approach is more conspicuous. If the descriptive mode has its center outside the things referred to, and the symbolic mode elevates a thing into an ideal being, the imitative mode describes things critically from inside themselves. From this point of view, Kant's wide use of "alienated" language material underscores inadequacies in the attitude toward persons and objects in question.

At times, Kant carries this "translation into language" even into the area of syntax. An interesting example in this connection is the expression "bei Ausübung des berühmten Blicks von der Wartburg" (370) (in the performance of the famous look from the Wartburg). Linguistically, we can describe this construction as a violation of the collocational rules for "Blick" and "Ausübung"; its function is to imitate by grammatical means the typical sightseer's pose, thereby satirizing underlying attitudes.

Other expressions along this line are "sich Phantasie anschaffen" ("to get imagination" 356), "so ein dickes Buch steht dir gut" ("such a thick book looks good on you" 18), "hier drüben" ("here over there" 200); the latter, a self-contradictory local adverbial phrase, expresses that Riek, a former classmate of Iswall's, although living in West Germany, still takes East Germany as his real point of reference. The clash between incompatible connotations is a source of satirical humor for Kant; by saying that students were "delegated for the reception of cultural heritage" ("delegiert zur Entgegennahme von Kulturerbe," 370), he exposes the mechanical attitude of handling culture like a commodity.

The examples given here are related to what has been called "ethopoeia" in the traditional classification of figures of speech; in Kant's work, however, they are not isolated figures of speech but expression of an underlying principle: the "monkey" Iswall, from whose point of view everything is perceived, imitates parodistically — in his observations, in his reflections, and even in the way he remembers people talk — the very objects he is referring to; the result is that all characters resemble Iswall and each other in some way, and many of the characters occurring only in one episode are outright caricatures of that for which they stand: for example, the prune salesman, the Nestroy actor, the bishop, the theology professor, the old university president, the conservative student representative, several writers satirized in the Writers' League Meeting; but also more important figures, such as the teachers Völschow and Angelhoff.

Most of the characters sound at times more like Iswall than like themselves. Thus, Iswall's brother-in-law is wittier than he perhaps should be (154, 224); Iswall's boss makes puns like those of his apprentice (44); even Filter, the somewhat simple, but hearty hillbilly, "has gotten imagination," as he himself puts it (356); and Rose Trullesand, an otherwise simple, good-natured girl, is almost a match for Iswall, as far as witticisms are concerned (440 f.). Thus, the contours of the characters may become a bit blurred at times — but this blurring serves only to sharpen the prevailing mood of dialectical humor.

As mentioned above, the differences between description, dialog, and inner monolog are blurred by the fact that everything is, in the end, a reflection of Iswall's subjectivity. Thus, humorous inadequacy — or over-adequacy — is found both in the language used by a character and in the language of Iswall's reflections. The following short example shows the transition from objective report to subjective evaluation by means of imitation: "Sie [die Postkarte] kam aus Kassel, wo es der Frau seit vierzehn Tagen gutging." ("The postcard came from Kassel, where the lady was doing fine since two weeks ago," 194; compare also 21 and 177.) Thus Kant converts a given language material such as the probable postcard sentence "I have been in Kassel for two weeks and am doing fine" into a description expressing subjective evaluation: "the lady was doing fine since two weeks ago."

Kant uses an upstart's own favorite phrase "jetzt ja" to form the satiric name a "Jetzt-ja-Mann" ("now-that-we-can-afford-it" man, 269). One might be curious enough to ask if the proper names in the *Aula* are more than just names of characters. There have indeed been far-reaching speculations: the extreme was probably the interpretation of the hero's name as a cryptographic consent to the Berlin Wall — *Iswall* equalling "There *is* a *wall*." This assumption is not supported by anything in the novel. There is clearly something suggested, however, in the name of Riek's inn "Zum toten Rennen" ("The Dead Race," 179, 194). Iswall himself associates "Totes Rennen" with "Toter Hund," and the inn's street address, "Sechslingstwiete," with "Silberlingstwiete" (Street of the Silver Shekels). Still another example is the student named "Blank"; he is an activist (a distinguished worker at his last job); but, although he is seen on a whole as a positive character, he remains rather colorless or "blank" in the novel (277). There may or may not be more to Blank's name than just a name; but one thing is evident: the unproblematic socialist hero Blank is a minor character, Kant choosing the more problematic Iswall as his central character.

Humorous contrast

In the previous section I mentioned mixtures of stylistic levels: the apparent stylistic inadequacy was shown to point humorously at and to unresolved conflicts. Understatement and overstatement, as well as other forms of irony, by implying some type of contrast, serve the same purpose.

The most prevalent stylistic features used by Kant are those of enumeration and variation. Frequently Kant gives a list of concrete details (184, 219, 393, 121 — the latter example climaxing in a threefold rhyme). One encounters a cluster of metaphors, all taken from the same metaphorical field, where Kant-Iswall plays variations on the comparison of love and wine, developing a humorous allegory (110); and photography as the "art of distortion" is exemplified on two pages (368 ff.).

Among the names and paraphrases introduced in Iswall's imagined speech about Jakob Filter's high administrative job, one finds *oberster Waldhüter* (Chief Guardian of the Forest), *Ministerialer* (State Department Official), *Bürokrat* (Bureaucrat), *Schemelreiter* (Swivel-Chair Rider), *Aktenkommandeur* (Commander of Files), *Generalstäbler* (Staff-Officer), *Verwalter* (Administrator), *Hauptabteilungsleiter* (Department Head), *Schemelkapitän* (Swivel-Chair Captain), *Anleiter* (Trainer), and the further phrases *vom Revierförster zum Papierförster* ("from forest ranger to paper-work ranger") and *Lenkst du das Harzsammeln, bist du Chef aller Birkenwasserzapfer?* ("Do you direct sap-collecting, or are you the head of all collectors of birchtree sap?" 358–361). Kant uses these derogatory names and phrases in reference to a man who is otherwise pointed out as being the shining example of a "good" administrator. The central term here, *bureaucrat*, is humorously varied, and its ironic use is probably directed at "real-life" bureaucrats.

Iswall tries to gain clarity about his own past by using a series of metaphors; but he is not sure if he is using the right names for what he is trying to do:

> Der gute Robert Iswall zieht aus, um den bösen Robert Iswall in den Sand zu legen, Punktmachen nennt er das, reinen Tisch, rein Schiff, Schulden tilgen, und er weiß zugleich doch nicht, ob das die rechten Namen sind. (408)

> The good Robert Iswall rides out in order to conquer the bad Robert Iswall; he calls it settling a score, clearing the table, cleaning the ship, paying off debts; and yet, at the same time he does not know if these are the right names. (408)

A similar effect is created in the preceding enumeration and in the sequence of questions following the above.

The enumerations and combinations used by Kant are often paradoxically condensed. The phrase "politische Notwendigkeit und List Roberts" (304) ("political necessity and Robert's trickery") is the converse of the classical rhetorical figure, "hendiadyoin" — the artificial separating of a single term into two parts; in this case, the unity of the two factors is problematic. Kant seems to allude to Hegel's principle that historical necessity "tricks" people into furthering progress by exploiting even the vices and character flaws they may have; and since the context makes it clear that the "political necessity" is rather questionable in this case, no synthesis is suggested; instead, the unreconciled thesis and antithesis keep pointing to a conflict.

Thus talking about and around a phenomenon rather than actually finalizing the name of the object in question focuses attention on the problem itself, but does not give any direct answer to it. Indeed, the complexity of human life finds adequate expression in Kant's open style.

Preference for the concrete

In most of the preceding examples, Kant enumerates a series of concrete details rather than leaving the matter on the level of a general term. This observation can be generalized: Kant shows a preference for the concrete rather than the abstract; he speaks of persons rather than of institutions, of thoughts and feelings of individuals rather than of group events (compare 285–298). Abstractions like "democracy," "Party," "the new man," and "progress," are usually ironized as not capturing the whole reality, or even as camouflaging partial failures in the present system. As for the dialectical unities of the concrete and the abstract, of the individual and the general, of the subjective and the objective, Kant questions any naive deduction that would not do justice to the paradoxes which constitute reality.

The relationship between "new truths" and "seemingly remote, insignificant details" is made the subject of a reflection Iswall has about transitions from one stage of his life to the next:

> neue, umstürzende Wahrheiten enthüllten sich in scheinbar abgelegenen Details . . .. Aber auch die freundlichen Enthüllungen hatten sich ohne Tusch und Feuerwerk vollzogen, oft eher komisch . . .. (383 f.)

37

new, shaking truths revealed themselves in seemingly remote, insignificant details . . .. But also the pleasing revelations had taken place without fanfares and fireworks, frequently in a rather comical manner . . ..

Kant's oscillation between inadequate terms, his staying with concrete examples, pointing beyond the objects referred to, and general openness are not just camouflage; it is in itself a testimony of one person's awareness of the corruption and corruptibility of language, and at the same time an attempt at keeping language honest.

Formal style vs. elements of dialect, slang, and spoken language

At first glance, Kant's style, especially in the reflective passages, appears to be on the traditional medium of cultivated, literary prose with high or low style interspersions of humor. Low style is comprised primarily of spoken language, dialect, slang, and Party jargon; while high style is mainly comprised of formal, archaic, or poetic style. Although the latter direction is taken less frequently than the former, it is worthwhile to start with a consideration of formal and poetic elements.

Elements of formal style

In one scene, Iswall pictures himself as a "Festredner" (celebration speaker) and imagines himself addressing a typical convocation audience. This passage contains only a description of the audience and the long-drawn opening lines of a speech, but it is an effective parody of any "Festrede," with an abundance of anaphors, quotations, Latin interspersions, solemn archaic forms and expressions, a dominance of nominal constructions, and the typical commonplace praises of where the speech is being delivered (8 f.).

There are many more parodistic speeches, some of them quite extensively reported and commented upon: thus, the welcoming speech of the university president extends over more than three pages (66–70). This speech is another satire on the perennial nuisance of ceremonial addresses and convocation speeches, and, in addition, an attack on reactionary and overly-specialized, scholarly attitudes. This university president, also a professor, has lived only for the advancement of his small field in geology, and is so used to looking at vast time intervals that it is humorously adequate when he refers to the Reformation Age as "only recently, in the twenties and thirties of the sixteenth century" (67); and even his intentional puns on expressions of his own field are too contrived to be really funny. Other satirized elements in this speech are, again, long-winding sentences, the use of scholarly quotation, the use of Latin formulas, and archaic language. These stylistic features accompany and underscore what the content of the speech brings out quite clearly: namely, that this professor is an arrogant, narrow-minded, and somewhat pathetic representative of the old middle class. Much the same can be said for the speeches or the talks of the student representative (209-215), the bishop (396-400), and the theology professor (25-28).

If poetic language is used, there is always ironical implication:

> Blast fort den — na ja, seien wir mal nicht so — edlen Rauch der Warnow und Orient, und pustet und hustet herbei die Sondermischung, den Selbstgebauten und ach, die Gabe der Freunde, den lieblichen Machorka. (288)

> Blow away the — well, let's not be too picky — noble smoke of the Warnow and Orient, and huff and puff hither the special blend, the home-grown, and, ah! the gift of the friends, the lovely, sweet Machorka. (288)

Here, chain-smoker Iswall sings a hymn of praise to several tobaccos, alluding parodistically to Homer's epics and to classical German poetry by means of rhythm (almost two perfect hexameters), choice of words, and syntactic features typical of epic diction. There is a sharp contrast between the initial dactylic rhythm and the final trochees, between the poetic frame and the prosaic interjection, as well as a clash between highly poetical and rather trivial words; and there is the starkly ironic *lieblich* with reference to the Russian Machorka — a humorous play on the persisting, though slightly improved, problems with goods that are officially regarded as luxuries.

Elements of dialect, slang, and spoken language

As the last example again shows, there are elements of many styles and registers in the *Aula*, ranging from poetic style to slang and dialect. Kant does not attempt to use these different levels of language in a purely naturalistic way, but combines elements of various levels into new, humorous units, or distorts a specific style into a caricature. Taking stylistic consistency and adequacy as our point of reference, we can say that he estranges things, persons, and events comically through unexpected turns of language: common objects are treated in high style, and vice versa; and the levels of style or different styles are intermixed.

Slang and colloquial language are mainly employed in the frequent dialogs of the *Aula*; this use of lower language levels is particularly prevalent in the conversations between the four students at the Workers' and Peasants' College. Thus, the first encounter of Iswall and his best friend Trullesand with the "Aula" of their university is described in a mixture of slang and chivalric motifs:

> "...die haben gesagt, Arbeiter-und-Bauern-Fakultät, und nun sieh dir das an. Hier kannst du doch nur mit einem Pferd reinreiten, Steigbügel aus Gold, und da vorn auf dem Thron sitzt die Königin und schmeißt mit Rosen nach dir."
> Trullesand gefiel das. "Und denn linst du ihr von oben, von dein Roß, in den Ausschnitt, und denn wird dir schwindlig, und die Knappen fangen dich auf und geben dir Neckar zu saufen, weil sie auf so was vorbereitet sind." (9)

> "...they said, Workers' and Peasants' College, and now look at this. Here you can only ride in on a horse, stirrups of gold; and there in front on the throne sits the queen, throwin' roses at you."
> Trullesand liked that. "And then from above, from up on your ol' steed, you peek down into her dress, and then you get all dizzy, and the pages catch you and give you Neckar to guzzle since they're prepared for things like that." (9)

In this example, the spoken language elements constitute a hilarious parody of chivalric culture — a culture which has, from the beginning, due to its high-strung ideals and its insistence on form, invited parodies.

Elements of spoken language, dialect, and even slang are particularly prevalent in Trullesand's speech. His account of a visit to a dentist is a gold-mine of these elements: one finds redundancy, introduction of sentences by *und* (and), asyndetic sequences, preference for parataxis, verbless sentences, indirect speech without introductory *daß*, emphatic change from the past into the present tense, interjections indicating gestures, and unfinished sentences; examples of colloquial vocabulary are *Spachtel* (spatula), for the dentist's tool, *rüber* instead of *herüber*, and the adverb *man* (37–39).

Sometimes Trullesand does not make the distinction between accusative and dative. For example, instead of "Hände weg von Omas *Eingemachtem*" Trullesand says "Hände weg von Omas *Eingemachtes!*"; instead of "Sorg *dich* man nicht," "Sorg *dir* man nicht" (36).

Also, one finds the starkly colloquial possessive constructions with the possessive adjective as in "dem Pastor seine Tochter" (126) and "Rockefellern seine Brille" (319). These constructions are the more noticeable since Kant uses at other places even the stiff construction of preposed genitive with article to express a possessive relationship, e. g. in the imagined book title "Des Zuckers Spur" (*The Sugar's Trace*, 265). The genitive is usually avoided in spoken German; and, even in written German, the preposed possessive genitive with article reeks of bookishness. In this case, Kant makes fun of the novel "Die Spur der Steine" by Erik Neutsch. Similarly, a Party official is satirized by his describing the musical "Die Blume von Hawai" ("The Flower of Hawaii") as "eine Operette, in der eines unterdrückten Volkes Not besungen wurde," ("an operetta in which a suppressed people's plight is sung," 394). The genitive construction, together with "die Not besingen," an archaic poetic phrase, ridicules in its context a dogmatic attitude toward the arts.

Elements of spoken language and slang are, however, not entirely restricted to dialog; they also occur interspersed in Iswall's reflections. Iswall uses the curse "Verflucht noch mal" ("Damn it" 105); and, about a French dog, we learn: "Der biß keinen, der begrüßte jeden ... als hätte er jahrelang mit ihm an den Eiffelturm gepinkelt." ("This dog wouldn't bite anyone, he greeted everyone ... as though he had weeweed at the Eiffel Tower with him for years," 42.) Slang and strong language are rather carefully measured ingredients, adding a flair of boyish boisterousness to otherwise serious reflections and dialogs. More frequently, Iswall and the other students avoid taboo words and strong expressions.

In this connection, one might mention Kant's use of animal imagery, a common feature of popular style: for example, "ich Büffel" ("I'm such a buffalo"), "mein Brummen" ("my growling"), "hereingetrampelt kommen" ("to come trampling in"), "Brummen" ("growling"), "kein Büffel" ("no buffalo"), all on page 170.[38] Furthermore, there are several stories centering around animals: the fatal error of the Irish setter Iraque (while trying to catch a locomotive by the "leg," he is killed) is paralleled with the behavior of a minister who, while waiting in the church door for approaching Russian soldiers, is killed by them (46 f.; 49).

In the use of popular language elements, Kant at times does not avoid faded and cliché-like metaphors ("unter donnerndem Beifall" — "with thundering applause," 28; "Heidenspektakel" — "hullabaloo," 181; "dröhnen" — "with a booming voice," instead of "laut reden" — "to talk loudly," 8); trite exaggerations like "Es dauerte eine Ewigkeit" ("It lasted an eternity," 26) and "im Höllentempo" ("very fast," 131); or other expressions that remind strongly of trivial literature: "[er sagte] empört" ("he said with utter indignation," 36) and "stiefeln" ("to stalk along") instead of "laufen" (36, 329, 333). Whether Kant "overdid it" in these and a few other instances will remain a question of personal taste. In my opinion, they are at most only minor flaws in an otherwise brilliantly polished style — flaws which might well be excused altogether as simply being typical of the character "Affe Iswall."

As for the spelling of spoken language and slang, Kant rarely departs from normal orthography; dialect variations like *wat* and *ick* instead of the regular *was* and *ich*, respectively, are not used consistently but rather incidentally, for the purpose of local color. In a conversation between Trullesand and Iswall, Trullesand uses *ich* and *ick* interchangeably (e.g., 51); and in the story of his visit to the dentist, there is only one occurrence of *wat* but eight of *was*, this one being found in the idiom "wat liegt an?" (37), an idiom which is used leitmotivically in Trullesand's speech.

To summarize the above observations about elements of spoken language, dialect, and slang: far from naturalistic imitation, Kant's style includes carefully measured elements from non-literary kinds of speech: one finds only few phonetic changes, but more examples of dialect syntax, and even more frequently and noticeably one runs across words and phrases from non-literary styles.

The functions of mixing stylistic levels

The functions of mixing stylistic levels and using "inadequate" expressions remain to be discussed. What has thus far been said about Iswall's insecurity, can now be generalized: in all of the speeches of the young students, there is a boyish shying away from the "right words." Kant lets Trullesand, Iswall's best friend, state this expressly: " — aber heute, wo wir zehn Jahre älter sind und vor den richtigen Worten nicht mehr so viel Angst haben, ..." (" — but today, where we are ten years older and are not so much afraid of the right words anymore, ..." 454).

Together with the personal development of the students, there is a social development which can be described in part as acculturation. In the case of Trullesand, we see the linguistic reflection of this social process. Whereas Iswall, being an avid reader and a self-educated man, has full command of the German language when entering college, his fellow student Trullesand does not, although he tries hard. The latter's struggle with language includes tackling the more complicated syntactical structures and applying the terminology of dialectical materialism. Thus, his speeches end up a hilarious mixture of hearty, witty, and folksy language, interwoven with reminiscences of his former carpenter's trade, and interspersed with elements of formal language and Party German. Thus, his versions of the marxist lectures he has read or attended are masterpieces of dialectical humor (cf. 37 f., 42 f., 129, 146, 166 ff., 172).

Trullesand himself — as well as his classmates — finally overcomes the language barrier: having earned his doctor's degree in Chinese during seven years at Peking University, Trullesand uses his old jargon more as an allusion to former times to show that he did not forget or despise what was good during those times.

Kant exploits in a humorous way situations in which the children of the "workers and peasants," rising above their former low educational level, lack the mastery of the language required in their new environment. It is a recurring motif that one of them is humiliated by a member of the formerly ruling class, the "bourgeois" remaining superior through his mastery of cultural tools: Trullesand proves inferior to the dentist, the culminating point being that he is unable to detect a logical fallacy in the latter's argumentation, which causes Trullesand to plan to study philosophy (38); in a German lesson about Keller's "Abendlied," the students struggle for an expression of what they feel (which is more honest and to the point, incidentally, than what the old professor is used to seeing in that poem, 112–115); and, in a student body election, the inexperience and laconicisms of the proletarian students cause the audience to roar with laughter and allow a glib reactionary to amuse himself at their expense (206 ff.).

In all of the above, Kant is emphatic about socialism giving the formerly suppressed classes full access to those areas of human experience formerly restricted to the upper classes; and one notes Kant's pride in claiming that the underprivileged of the old society will make use of their new status.

This is not to say, however, that Kant overlooks the problems involved in the process of "acculturation," as seen in the expression "sich an Goethe heranmachen" ("to sneak up to Goethe" 370). This expression is coined in connection with the proletarian students visiting the Eisenach Bach festival, to which they are delegated "for the purpose of receiving cultural heritage." This expression is at the same time an acknowledgment of Goethe's rank, a criticism of the official administrative approach to culture, and an example of the difficulties involved in gaining access to cultural tradition.

The difficulties previously mentioned include the following problem: these students, as representatives of the "victorious working-class," are not called upon to grow uncritically into an established cultural tradition, but rather to select only what is progressive in existing culture, or are even called upon to participate in a cultural revolution. This is why the term "acculturation" is insufficient; and this is why Kant-Iswall's attitude to language is so dialectical. The permanent struggle for the "right words" accompanies and reflects the difficult process of emancipation.

It is interesting in this connection to mention that Kant seems to allude satirically to Stalin's treatise "Zu einigen Fragen der Sprachwissenschaft" by speaking of "linguistic riddles finally solved" by Stalin (401). In this treatise Stalin claims that language, e.g. the Russian language, is chiefly a neutral tool of communication which does not influence the socio-economic system in which it is used. Kant, however, suggests that language is more actively involved with certain contents; and he seems to warn that the proletarian students, while acquiring and mastering the traditional higher levels of language, might also take on some of the spirit and ideology contained therein. What was said about the dialectics of the old and the new in connection with the "Affe" motif, can be repeated with respect to language: in and through language more of the old is surviving than the dogmatic optimist would like to believe; and, if this be true, even the "right words" of the communist ideology may be wrong — that is, if these "right words" do not reflect socio-economic developments as they really are.

As a last function of Kant's stylistic mixtures and his wide use of colloquial style, the entertainment aspect should be mentioned. Parodistic contrast of styles and effective use of colloquial style are important constituents of the *Aula*'s humor, and explain in part the wide appeal this book has had in both East and West Germany. Kant writes in popular fashion — which is one of the requirements of Socialist Realism — but, on close inspection, he seems to fulfill this requirement somewhat ironically. The following sections will present more material to prove that Kant's style is more than just entertaining, and more than just Socialist Realism.

Language of Party and bureaucracy

In this section, the outstanding elements of Party language will be presented, again without claim to exhaustiveness, but with the goal of at least touching upon its important formal characteristics and functional aspects.

Satire on Party jargon

As in the case of colloquial language, Party language is almost never used in its own right, that is, as an existing jargon used in certain social contexts, but it is almost invariably exposed as being somehow "inadequate": if Kant wants to speak seriously about progress in East Germany or about the sincere communist convictions of his heroes, he resorts usually to general terms, understatements, or implications.

In one of the rare instances in which Kant directly criticizes the use of marxistic vocabulary, Kant speaks of "all-purpose expressions like main link, new type, higher level, basic, basis, and non-antagonistic contradiction" ("Allzweckausdrücke wie Hauptkettenglied, neuer Typus, höhere Stufe, grundlegend, Basis und nichtantagonistischer Widerspruch,"

178). These terms have a well-defined meaning within socialist theory, but as "all-purpose expressions" they become hypocritical stereotypes. The term *neuer Typus* deserves special attention: the other terms very rarely if ever reoccur in the novel, but *neuer Typus, neuer Typ,* and *das Neue* are used several times. It combines the meaning of the others, referring to anything in a socialistic society that is basically different from any time before, since the change of the "basis" moved history to a "higher level" on which only "non-antagonistic contradictions" are possible. Meibaum exclaims in one situation that if he is a bureaucrat, then he is one of the "new type" (237). In cases like these, one must understand the background of the word *new.*

In one of the places where Iswall pictures himself delivering his "Aula" speech, he has a group of Party officials call the expression *to delegate someone* explicitly "an invention with which one can persuade each and every one, even if the person doesn't want to be persuaded" ("eine Erfindung, mit der man einen jeden überreden kann, auch wenn er nicht will, und sie nennen es: delegieren," 366). In this case the blunt of the criticism is taken away by the fact that in this particular situation the persuasion serves the best of the person involved.

Usually Kant employs indirect methods to expose the negative aspects of Party jargon. Thus, it is the context that ironizes the terms *Abweichung* (deviation), *Schwankung* (inconstancy), and *weltanschaulich* (ideological), (147).

The language of Trullesand gives numerous examples of comical criticism of marxistic terms, e.g. the application of the theory of imperialism to a grocery store owner by means of etymology: "An seiner Tür steht 'Kolonialwaren'; der will seine Kolonien wieder. Diese Krämer sind alle Ausbeuter." ("That guy still has 'Kolonialwaren' on his door — stuff from the colonies; he wants his colonies back. These shopkeepers are all exploiters," 152.) At other places Trullesand delivers hilarious treatises on topics like marriage, psychology, and the form-content problem (129, 166 f., 233 f.). His simplifications of already simplified and popularized marxism, as well as his folksy sense of humor, work together to achieve effective, even if involuntary, parodies on Party jargon.

The most daring indirect method of implicit criticism is refutation of communist propaganda by political reality. If one reads, for example, about "eternal friendship" with the comrades in China, one knows how short this eternity has thus far been: "... weil in China die Genossen gesiegt haben und wir auf ewig Freundschaft miteinander geschlossen haben,"

("... because in China the comrades have been victorious and because we have made an eternal friendship with them." 308).

In the same scene one finds another type of contrast which confronts ideology with features of the situation itself, if the situation is looked upon with common sense. A Chinese scholarship offering is called "noble" ("hochherziges Anerbieten aus Peking," 310), but the rather restrictive and confining terms of the scholarship itself serve to ironize this praise. The irony is intensified by the use of high, archaic style (*hochherzig* and *Anerbieten* instead of *großzügig* and *Angebot*).

The lack of originality in East German propaganda style is mocked in the tentative title of an article against the West German "Kringel-Konzern" ("Springer-Concern," in disguise), which varies Fontane's famous saying about the role of European missionaries in Africa: "Sie sagen Pressefreiheit und meinen Kattun," ("They say freedom of the press and mean cotton," 33). Again, one should not overlook the other levels of meaning in this example of dialectical humor: for example, Kant subscribes in principle to the criticism of the West German press giant alluded to.

Also, hyphenated twin formulas, a typical feature of marxistic jargon, are ironized in themselves (like "wachsam-zufrieden," vigilant-pleased, 114), or by their context (like "praktisch-poetisch," practical-poetical, 245).

The language of the administrated world

Frequently, the words and constructions typical of Party jargon belong at the same time to the language of administration, carrying with them the connotation of impersonality. The word *Kader* (cadre) is, in socialistic usage, the technical term for those persons who form the backbone of the Party and of other organizations in socialist countries. Whenever this word is used, it suggests a mechanical attitude toward the people in question (30, 31; *Arbeiterkader*, 158). Openly de-humanizing is the word *Elemente* (elements), used for refugees from the GDR (265).

This mechanical, impersonal attitude is reinforced by a series of other devices. On the syntactic level, for example, one encounters relatively many passive constructions and omissions of the agent: for example, "es wurde beschlossen," ("It was decided," 52). As far as figurative use of language is concerned, one notices the use of technological terms: *sich einschalten, staatliche Stellen einschalten* (158), *herausarbeiten, Schalthebel der Wirtschaft* (267). The etymology of the expression *mit Auslaufen* (used in place of *zum Ende* in Meibaum's telegram — 7, 8, 9, 18) likewise points to the field of technology. Although this technical etymology might normally go unnoticed, it is activated in a context of continuous ironizations.

When talking about a band, Kant lets the speaker poke fun at the obsessive use of technical names for non-technical objects: "Die vier Turbos. Kommt wahrscheinlich von Turbine. Festlicher Ausklang mit Geheule. . . ." ("The Four Turbos. Probably comes from turbine. Festive conclusion with howling. . . ." 459). Machine names like *Traktor, Dynamo,* and *Lokomotive* are indeed favorite names for sport teams in East Germany (335).

In an instructive small episode, Meibaum reformulates a relatively spontaneous utterance into Party jargon: when caught off guard by the mention of a problematic student, he says: "Über den sollte bei der Abschlußfeier besser nicht gesprochen werden; ich meine, über solche Elemente sollte auf keinen Fall gesprochen werden." ("It would be better if that one wasn't spoken of at the concluding celebration; I mean such elements should in no case be spoken of," 265). Both sentences show the preference for the impersonal passive; in Meibaum's self-correction, the impersonal attitude is reinforced by the replacement of the colloquial *der* by *solche Elemente* and by the sharpening of the mild negation *besser nicht* into the strong rejection *auf keinen Fall*. The emphatic *auf keinen Fall* occurs more than once in this passage, as do the strong affirmations *völlig richtig!* (exactly right) — expressions of a thinking which knows only all or nothing. In this scene, Meibaum may be only pretending that he has strong feelings against the person in question, since this person may really be a communist undercover agent to the West instead of someone who fled from East Germany; but even if this were the case, it would not affect the observations about his language.

Nominal style, especially in the form of a bloated verb paraphrase containing a nominalization, is another feature of administrative language which Kant ridicules, e.g. *zur Sprache bringen* instead of *sagen* or *erwähnen* (equivalent to *to make mention of* vs. *to mention*, 53). In particular, nominalizations with the suffix *-ung* are exposed, as in the phrases *dem Vorschlag mit Ablehnung begegnen* (the proposal meets with rejection, 206) and *das Beispiel in Anwendung bringen* (corresponding roughly to an English expression like *by way of application of the example*, 207).

The -*ung* formations even become the topic of a conversation which Iswall has with his wife; fittingly, the discussion gets started with the bureaucratic key word *Verordnung* (order, official regulation), which is playfully substituted for Luther's word *Gebot* in his version of the Christmas story (19). This conversation prompts reflections by Iswall, the end being stylistic variations on the theme "death notice": first, the sad event is expressed in normal, conversational style; then it is given the stereotyped form of a public announcement; finally, it is translated into bureaucratic German, characterized by its abundance of -*ung* words (24). What might at first appear as a purist's objection to bureaucratic German goes beyond the realm of the aesthetic; the inherent danger or even presence of inhumanity in any administrative system is pointed out.

Criticism of -*ung* formations is also found in Strittmatter's *Ole Bienkopp*, again in connection with Party bureaucracy.[39] As far as the word and concept of *Verordnung* is concerned, there is an interesting parallel in Alexander Solzhenitsyn's *Ein Tag im Leben des Iwan Denissowitsch*:

"... Das wußten doch schon die Alten, daß die Sonne mittags am höchsten steht."
"Die Alten wohl!" antwortete der Käptn barsch. "Seitdem ist aber eine Verordnung erlassen worden, wonach die Sonne um ein Uhr am höchsten zu stehen hat."
"Wer hat diese Verordnung erlassen?"
"Die Sowjetmacht!"
...Ist es wirklich so, daß die Sonne bereits ihren Verordnungen gehorcht?[40]

"... That the sun is highest at noon — that was even known by the ancients."
"The ancients — yes," answered the Capt'n curtly. "But since then, a regulation has been issued according to which the sun has to be highest at one o'clock."
"Who has issued this regulation?"
"The Soviet Power!"
...Has it really come to that, that even the sun obeys their regulations?

Common to both Kant's and Solzhenitsyn's works is their criticism of bureaucracy; the differences in the treatment of the same motif, however, show the differences between the positions of these authors: while Solzhenitsyn attacks with strident sarcasm Stalin's systematic terror behind the phenomenon of bureaucracy, Kant plays humorously with the abuses as well as the necessities of administration. After all, Iswall's "Arbeiter-und-Bauern-Fakultät" came visibly into being only by an administrative act — a "Verordnung"; and this central example of newness and progress in East Germany is actually the topic of the conversation referred to above.

Satirical new coinages

In addition to criticizing Party jargon by the methods described above, Kant creates for the same critical purpose words in analogy to existing words. Satirical is the construction *saftige Entlarve,* with the slang coinage *Entlarve* being used by a journalist to describe a propaganda project against a West German target (33). Equally satirical is *Rückwärtsler,* formed in analogy to *Vorwärtsler* (roughly, *regressivist* and *progressivist,* 459).

Formations like *Dok-Film* instead of *Dokumentarfilm* (33), *Orgstud* instead of *organisiertes Selbststudium* (132), and *Infra,* used as an abbreviation for *Aussprachen über individuelle Fragen* (discussions of personal questions, 133), parody the trend toward excessive abbreviation and over-organization.

Compound nouns with *-mensch* as second constituent seem to be a productive pattern in East German usage; Kant alludes to these formations and their inhuman mechanism of classification, using them excessively in connection with the West German "sewer rat" Grieper.[41]

In a few instances, there are grammatical differences between administrative or Party German and the other kinds of German. One example of this sort is the verb *orientieren auf,* used intransitively without the regularly required reflexive pronoun, namely in the idiomatic phrase *auf das Neue orientieren* (to get one's bearings from the new, 35; 45, 462). This peculiar grammatical form is found frequently in East German journals, political literature, etc.; and it is interesting to note that Kant has this form used by Party officials, adding in only one instance the reflexive pronoun (159).

Dogmatism as cause of inadequate Party jargon

It was stated at the beginning of this section that there is always something inadequate or incongruous about what is referred to here as Party jargon. One explanation is that Kant criticizes the inhumanity inherent in any bureaucratic system. One can go one step further, however, and find the connection between bureaucratism and the basic inadequacy of socialist dogmatism. The underlying pattern of every dogmatism is this: all correct answers are given; now all one has to do is to fit a problem to the given solution, or to find a question for the answer. Wherever Kant encounters this attitude, he exposes it by means of dialectical humor; for he seems to believe in the basic correctness of the marxistic approach.

It is clear that a dogmatic can raise only rhetorical questions, pretending — or ultimately believing — that these are real questions. The very word *Frage* (question) serves as the core element of various idioms of dogmatic language, veiling deductive reasoning with the semblance of discussion, as is the case in the following monolog:

> Sehr richtig, ... was sollen Sie in Hannover? So muß man die Frage doch stellen. Aber man muß weiter fragen: Ist es richtig, daß ein Mensch wie Sie ohne Tätigkeit ist? Das ist natürlich nicht richtig. Unser Land braucht alle Hände. Aber braucht es nicht auch alle Köpfe? In der Tat braucht es sie. (30)

> Exactly right, ... what would you do in Hanover? That's the way one must ask the question. But one must ask further: is it right that a person like you is without a job? That is of course not right. Our country needs all hands. But doesn't it need all heads, too? As a matter of fact, it does need them. (30)

The preceding quote is taken from Iswall's admissions interview; and it is the dogmatic, yet in a way sympathetic teacher Völschow who is talking. His further contributions during this interview are a collection of the vices of dogmatic language. Adjectives like *echt* and *uralt* are characteristic of the "Jargon der Eigentlichkeit," as when he speaks of *echte Alternative* (true alternative). Furthermore, Völschow uses propaganda stereotypes like *unsere antifaschistisch-demokratische Staatsordnung* (our anti-fascistic-democratic political system), a term which is out of place, at least in that situation, as is the socialist text-book abstraction "now the age-old opposition between power and intelligence is removed." To prove a point he alludes to a technical term of socialist politics, *Intelligenzpakete* (intelligence parcels), or quotes "Comrade Stalin." Typical are also formulas of self-criticism like "Ich präzisiere also" (30) ("Let me specify"; similarly, "Ich korrigiere mich wie folgt" — "I correct myself as follows," 112, 114). Instead of the promised, more precise formulation, Völschow offers only hilarious tautologies.

The two other Party functionaries through whose language the dogmatic aspect of the Party jargon is ironized are Dean Meibaum and the Latin teacher Angelhoff. The former lacks the redeeming grace of enthusiasm and idealism, which makes Völschow a "sympathetic stalinist," if such can be said of anyone; Meibaum is only the cold "apparatchik," complaining at one time that he did not find any personal contact with his students, and at the same time still addressing his former pupil Iswall as *Genosse* (Comrade, 263). Angelhoff, on the other hand, is a fierce dogmatic only at the surface, hiding beneath reactionary attitudes.[42]

To give a few examples of Meibaum's style of speaking and thinking: when talking with Iswall about a sugar thief in the post-war austerity time, he analyzes the situation with the clichés "Rudimente eines pervertierten Solidaritätsbegriffes" (remnants of a perverted solidarity concept), "falscher Kameradschaftsgeist der faschistischen Wehrmacht" (false camaraderie of the fascist army), "Angehöriger der Arbeiterklasse, die nunmehr Herr der Werke und Werte ist" (member of the working-class, who is by this time master of production and property, 263 f.). The analysis of the sugar theft in abstract, ideological terms is even more ridiculed: Meibaum goes on to say that he would have expected the converted sugar thief to become a hammer thrower (the sugar thief had thrown sugar sacks over a factory wall) since that sports discipline was "lagging far behind on the regional level" (146).

It is in keeping with Kant-Iswall's anti-dogmatic position that the term *Disziplin* receives negative connotations in its context (53); *iron Party discipline* was, after all, one of the central terms of the stalinist branch of communism. In a witty chat, Iswall suggests to his partner in conversation that the word *Intellektueller* is a derogatory term — which it was indeed in the times of Stalin, and probably under every régime with totalitarian tendencies (301).

The above observations confirm the interpretation that Kant is well aware of the specific danger of bureaucracy in his country, namely that the Party bureaucracy poses a threat to the individual and to the entire society in so far as it sanctifies its objective power with a dogma that cannot be questioned. The next section will present more evidence for this claim, investigating Kant's use of the language which is often regarded as the prime example of dogmatism — religious language.

Use of Religious Language and Religious Motifs

It is commonplace to say that the Bible is the most influential book in Western culture, having supplied thoughts and motifs, as well as stylistic features and idioms to both literary and everyday language. Biblical language and religious motifs have also found their way into Kant's *Aula*. The following discussion will be restricted to the semantic field of religious terms, i.e., to explicit references to established forms of religious beliefs in Kant's *Aula*. Both stylistic and ideological functions of this phenomenon will be dealt with here.

Luther's language in Kant's *Aula*

The *Aula* has frequent allusions to Luther's Bible translation, as well as several allusions to Luther himself. As for Luther's language, we find several of his striking coinages like *Ottern und Schlangengezücht* (293), *Löwengrube, Fresser und Säufer* (225), as well as other typical expressions such as *Stückwerk treiben* (366), *der lebendige Gott* (225), *reuiger Sünder* (418), *des lieben Nächsten* (439), *Auserwählte* (372), etc.

At other places, Kant uses syntactic and grammatical features of the Luther language. Word choice and diction remind one of Luther, as when, in analogy to attributes of God or Christ, he states about the hero's father:

[Sein Vater Paul Iswall] war heute für immer das, was er gestern gewesen war, würde sich nicht mehr ändern und durfte darum geglaubt werden. (412)[43]

[His father, Paul Iswall,] was today forever that which he had been yesterday; would never change and could therefore be believed.

Besides the words and grammatical features Kant borrowed directly from Luther's language, we find biblical expressions that have already become stock language, a distinction which cannot always be clearly drawn. It must be added that Kant shows a preference for this second type and that even his "direct" quotations are usually well-known.

In almost every one of the above quoted examples, the author introduces a humorous or ironical contrast to the religious term used, by either varying the expression itself and combining it with conflicting word material, or by creating a humorous inadequacy between what is said and what is suggested. As to his preference for conventionalized expressions, at least one reason is the stronger comical and satirical effect achieved by changing the unchangeable. The aesthetic function, we might say, is stronger in the parody of "genuine" Luther language, whereas the play with common stock puts more emphasis on the moral function. Construing a humorous contrast by varying a standing biblical phrase can be seen in the following: "der eine Nase hat zu riechen" (288); ("if any man have a nose to smell, let him smell"). The effect of this parodistic variation is the stronger since the point of reference is a stinking sewer creek.

The biblical expression "in Sack und Asche gehen" (to go in sack cloth and ashes) is comically modernized in the sentence "Vielleicht trug ich auch ein Gewand aus Sackleinen und kippte mir immerfort Asche über den Kopf!" (233); ("Perhaps I also wore a vestment of sackcloth and continuously dumped ashes over my head!"). Here are several contrasts between Luther's language and modern German. The only archaic word retained is *Gewand* (vestment, garment, raiment), the other words belong to normal style (*Kopf* instead of the biblical *Haupt*), technical terminology (*Sackleinen*), and even slang (*kippen* instead of the expected *streuen*). The verb *kippen*, in conjunction with *immerfort*, contains furthermore a gross exaggeration of the old Jewish mourning rite. Another example of stylistic clash between biblical language and slang is "Nimm dein Bett und wandle, und alles diese Dinger," ("Take up thy bed and walk, and all that stuff," 51); *und alles diese Dinger* is, incidentally, one of the favorite phrases of the person speaking.

Metaphorical use of secularized religious concepts

Religious terms occur in proverbial use, as in the proverb "Wenn man vom Teufel spricht, dann kommt er" ("If you speak of the devil, he will come,"), a proverb alluded to in the *Aula*. However, more interesting than the proverbial use is the metaphorical use of religious concepts such as *God, devil, hell, heaven, angel, miracle, sacrifice.* When the six students are delegated to the Bach festival, this trip is compared to the chosen ones going to heaven: " '. . .lassen Sie unsere sechs Auserwählten ohne Traktat in den Himmel fahren.' — So fuhren sie denn in den Himmel, . . ." (372).

Wunder (miracle) has, as a metaphor, the connotation of something illusionary or at least questionable (e.g. 104); and if the narrator imagines himself using the phrase *Wunder der Literatur* in his future speech, the pathos of that expression is criticized (16). For a girl student, her scholarship to China is like a "Wunder," as is her getting a passport and getting a husband — all of which come as a result of a Party meeting (305 f.). The religious term bears the connotation of naiveté, which is in this case only mildly satirized since the girl possesses redeeming qualities. For a reporter, it would be a real "miracle" if his newspaper editor would accept as much as half of his report (184). Iswall admits that he may use the word *Wunder* too much (392), and he does reject an unhistorical, visionary view of the past ("Historie im Schwärmerschein"), using the pun *Wunderkerzenlicht* (sparkler's light, miraculous candle light, 393). And yet, Iswall affirms the existence of "miracles" in connection with his friendship with Trullesand, underscoring the high value he attaches to such a friendship.

God and *devil* are used as psychological metaphors. It is the devil who tempts a poor teacher into a pedagogically fatal mistake (111); the devil tempts two boys to go so near the end of a roof that they have to be rescued (182); and it is the devil who must have initiated the betrayal of Trullesand by Iswall.

The first two examples given use the devil metaphor in a rather playful way; in the scene on the roof, a somewhat forced pun on the idiom "den Teufel an die Wand malen" introduces the devil, who is not only the personified temptation of showing off before a girl, but also "winks his eye" at Iswall, prompting a harmless erotic remark. A similar exaggeration is the threefold reference to the rescuer as *Engel* (183), and the word *Engelstat* for his deed (184).

The third example, the betrayal of a good friend, is one of the central conflicts of the entire novel; and there, the use of the devil metaphor is somewhat extended and differentiated. Kant over-emphasizes ironically the metaphorical character of this notion:

> Schade, daß ich nicht an den Teufel glaube; manchmal fehlt er mir. Gewisse Rechnungen gehen ohne ihn nicht auf. Da borge ich ihn mir dann, wie früher in der Schule den Zehner, wenn man dreizehn von sieben abziehen mußte. Wenn ich den Teufel in diese Geschichte einsetze, leihweise natürlich, dann geht sie so weiter: Der Teufel schickte ... den Genossen Wigg ... an die Fakultät und ließ ihn dort einen Brief aus Peking vorlegen. Zugegeben, es ist einigermaßen unglaubwürdig, daß er sich eines leitenden Genossen aus dem Staatsapparat und der chinesischen Freunde bedient haben soll, aber was am Teufel ist schon glaubwürdig.

> Too bad that I don't believe in the devil; sometimes, I could use him. Certain calculations don't work out without him. In that case, I borrow him, as I borrowed a ten in school when we had to subtract thirteen from seven. If I insert the devil into this story, then it continues like this: the devil sent ... Comrade Wigg ... to the College and there let him present a letter from Peking. Admittedly, it is somewhat unbelievable that he should have used a high-ranking comrade from the state government and our Chinese friends, but then, what is believable about the devil (430).

The humor here still is rather playful. Kant starts with the paradoxical remark that it is a pity that he doesn't believe in the devil; he later resolves this paradox by stating that the best term to describe certain coincidences is simply the word *diabolic*. The effect of this ironic reflexion is enhanced by Iswall's seemingly serious refutations of possible objections and misunderstandings. Kant spices this text with provocative allusions to the power of the Party bureaucracy and with allusions to China's relationship to other socialist countries; he hints at China's role as the "heretic" of the Communist block by rejecting this very idea as a sad misunderstanding of this figure of speech: "dies alles zugegeben, und auch die Gefahr eines Mißverständnisses, ich [...] sei der Meinung, des Teufels Spur führe nach Peking," ("admitting all of this, and also the danger of misunderstanding that I... was of the opinion that the devil's footprints were leading to Peking." 433).

Kant continues the justification of his using the devil metaphor, comparing the role of the devil in the life of Luther, Goethe's Faust, and Thomas Mann's Adrian Leverkühn; the end of these references are brief literary parodies:

> ... der Leipziger Doktor ist nur knapp davongekommen, der Musikant aus Kaisersaschern aber keineswegs, der ist zur Hölle gefahren und dazu hat's getönt, als wär's von Arnold Schönberg.... (433)

> ... the Leipzig doctor barely got away, the musician from Kaisersaschern not at all; this one went to Hell, to music which sounded as if it were by Arnold Schönberg.... (433).

Kant concludes the lenghty passage from which I have been quoting by re-emphasizing the evil consequences of Iswall's betrayal, and again he uses devil-and-hell imagery:

> ... nicht den Studienaufenthalt im beinahe fernsten Osten halte ich für einen Grund zu höllischem Gelächter, nicht einmal den Ehebund aus historischer Notwendigkeit halte ich dafür, aber das Ende der Freundschaft zwischen mir und Trullesand halte ich durchaus dafür, und es will mir nicht anders als unter Herbeiziehung des geborgten Teufels in den Kopf, daß ich... gesagt haben soll.... (433).

> ... the years of study in the almost farthest East, I don't regard as a reason for hellish laughter, not even the marriage ties on the basis of historical necessity, but the end of the friendship between me and Trullesand most definitively; and I can't explain it to myself other than through recourse to the borrowed devil that I... should have said.... (433).

What is described in one place as the work of the devil, is termed at three other places "lieber Gott spielen" (playing God, 52, 201, 422).

It is possible to see here a reflex of the theological thought that the basic temptation of man is to try to be like God, but this interpretation is not necessary since the expression "lieber Gott spielen" exists in German as an idiom. Kant takes this idiom and re-literalizes it ironically; namely, he continues to refer to the cause of these events as "der liebe Gott" (201, 202), and the girl, married more or less by decision of the Party meeting, is called "gottgegebene Frau" (God-given wife, 202). In all three occurrences of "playing God," Kant adds synonymically the expressions "Schicksal spielen" (playing Fate) and "historische Notwendigkeit spielen" (playing historical necessity). If used in isolation, "playing historical necessity" would have a more provocative ring; Kant tones it down by forming this construction in analogy to and as an extension of the two accompanying constructions, which, furthermore, have the authority of idioms. On the other hand, this trinity of terms occurs three times in the book, and a repeated understatement tends to become an emphasis.

It was already noted that Kant has a preference for variation and paraphrase. Thus, he changes the word *Teufel* to *Herr Teufel, Höllenkerl, geborgter Teufel, Leihteufel, Unterweltsphantom*, or compares the devil to a "Hilfskonstruktion" or "geborgter Zehner" (432 f.); Kant even goes into a historical digression and mentions *Fastnachts-, Sauf-, Zauber-, Spiel-, Jagd-, Hof-, Manns-, Weibs- und Hosenteufel*, (432). At other places, we find *der Böse* (430), *Luzifer* (22, 34), *Höllenfürst* (21), and *Beelzebub* (47). These paraphrastic variations and digressions distract from the thematic relevance of the devil image and tend to dissolve the ideas of temptation and evil into mere play — if these devices are not used for understatement.

It is in keeping with the generally indirect, even though satirical tone, that there are only few curse words to be found: for example a fourfold *gottverdammt*, curses which are actually only the imagined reaction of Raymond Chandler to an obnoxious cat ("das gottverdammte Stinktier," "that goddamn skunk") and its ridiculous owner, who wears a "Homespunanzug, dessen Schultern eine einzige gottverdammte Lüge waren" ("a homespun suit the shoulders of which were one goddamn lie," 226 f.).

In summary, one can say that Kant draws religious motifs directly from Luther's Bible translation or from the stock of idiomatic religious expressions already forming a part of language and that he combines, varies, or re-literalizes these religious motifs, extending at times metaphorical use of theological terms into ironical allegories. The effects

Kant achieves with the wide use of religious motifs are those of humor and satire; the satirical implications will be analyzed in some more detail in the following sections.

Religious language and motifs as a criticism of the church

In his ceremonial welcome address, the University President talks at length about the past history of the university, and even quotes an old decree initiating the Reformation: " 'Dat men schal aver dat gantze lant dat hillige evangelium lutter und rein predigen, und alle papistrie und ceremonien, so wedder Got weren, afdon' " (68). The reaction to this speech is typical of the attitude Kant seems to take towards established religion:

> "Wat haben wir denn mit Luthern? 'Wider die räuberischen Bauern' und alles diese Dinger!"...
> Was hatten sie mit Luthern? Das war nicht nur Trullesands Frage, und wenn sie zu dieser Stunde erfahren hätten, wie sehr sie es in der Folge noch zu tun bekommen sollten mit Luthern und manchem anderen, den sie nicht in ihr Bild von der neuen Zeit lassen wollten, dann wären sicher einige Plätze frei geblieben in der Robert-Blum-Straße dreiundzwanzig... (68)

> "What business do we have with this Luther? 'Wider die räuberischen Bauern,' and all that stuff!"...
> What business did they have with this Luther? That was not just Trullesand's question; and had they learnt at that hour how often they would be involved thereafter with this Luther and a number of other persons that they did not want in their image of the new era, then certainly several rooms would have stayed vacant at 23 Robert-Blum-Strasse... (68).

For Kant, religion seems to stand for reactionary mentality. Luther himself is, according to marxist doctrine, an ambivalent figure. As long as he fought against the established feudal system and as far as he provided ammunition for this fight, he is regarded as a positive, revolutionary figure; but when Luther turned away from the rebellious peasants and became a pillar of a new establishment and orthodoxy himself, he is seen negatively. Kant focuses on the negative aspect, as the above quotation indicates.

There are further references to "Doktor Martin Luther, diese verräterische Nachtigall" ("Doctor Martin Luther, that treacherous nightingale," 70); this expression alludes sarcastically to the popular praise of Luther as the "Wittembergische Nachtigall," which goes back to Hans Sachs' poem by the same name. Playing with the idiom *des Teufels sein* and using the theological idea originally expressed in it as a paradoxical metaphor for Luther's deserting the cause of the peasants, Kant states: "... der Bibeltranslator ... ist später aber doch des Teufels geworden und hat 'Wider die räuberischen und mörderischen Rotten der Bauern' geschrieben ..." (432 f.) ("... however, the biblical translator did later become one with the devil and wrote 'Against the thieving and murderous hordes of the peasants,'" a pamphlet fiercely denouncing the rebellious peasants, who claimed to be fulfilling the Reformer's pronouncements).

Speaking of J. S. Bach and his music, someone says "... ein sehr körperlich vorgestellter Gott, Höllenfurcht bis ins tiefste Bein." ("... a God conceived of as very corporeal, fear of Hell down to the last bone," 372); and the guide to the Wartburg "raunte ... eine Weile durchaus noch erschrocken vom Teufel, um dann fortzufahren, daß man mit den Mitteln der atheistischen Wissenschaft zu der Vermutung vorgedrungen sei, es habe sich wahrscheinlich um eine Halluzination des Bibelübersetzers gehandelt," (he whispered "for a while still really frightened of the devil; but then he continued that with the means of atheistic science, they had come as far as to conclude that what the Bible translator had experienced was probably a hallucination," 373).

"What business do we have with this Luther?" I have dwelt on this question of Kant's in order to show that he, in dealing with present-day church and religion, does not go beyond the realm of the medieval. However, this is not the whole answer yet; Kant parallels Völschow through several devices to Luther, suggesting certain similarities; our discussion will return to these parallels at a later point.

Referring to the War, Kant notes the possibility that Christians, despite their medieval belief in a *leibhaftiger Teufel*, may arrive at the correct view of a political question; but this case is isolated in the novel, and restricted furthermore by its dealing only with the past (47).

Medieval superstition becomes a metaphor or, more precisely, a whole field of metaphors for irrationalism (359 ff.). In another place, *Aberglaube* is linked to reactionary prejudice (70). The term *religiös* is implicitly said to be a step beyond *abergläubisch* (superstitious, 189), and religious imagery of *Opfer, Rauch, Himmel, Wunder,* and *Seele* (sacrifice, smoke, heaven, miracle, and soul, 85 f.) suggests a connection between religion and primitive, unjust social conditions: the passivity connected with the expectation of a miracle is rejected in favor of changing things by relying on one's own strength. Although this thought is developed on the level of a young boy daring to stand up against another, stronger boy, the implications are obvious.

In a more humorous sense, Kant calls certain formulas of his grammar teacher *Beschwörungsformeln* and *gläubige Sämannssprüche* (incantations and a yeoman's sowing charms, full of faith, 110); and about an unusual series of coincidences, he remarks: "Das stinkt doch geradezu nach Schwefel, da sieht man doch den Pferdefuß." ("That stinks outright of sulfur, there you can directly see the devil's club-foot." 431). But also these folklore elements about magic and the devil contribute to the image of religion outlined above.

As for the difference between atheism and religion, we find statements like "Und das mit dem Atheismus ist klar: Bei denen, die an den lieben Gott glauben, fliegt die Seele in den Himmel, und bei dem Dichter Gottfried Keller wird sie mit beerdigt." ("And that about atheism is clear: for those who believe in God, the soul flies to heaven, but the poet Gottfried Keller has the soul buried with the body," 113 f.). The author Kant does not necessarily identify with these simplifying and mockingly polemical statements, but he does nothing to differentiate this image of religion. His heroes do not envisage, for example, the possibility of understanding Adam and Eve mythologically (79 f.).

Kant satirizes the sentimental aspects of popular religion by using the diminutives *Englein im Himmel* (132) and *von Englein bewacht* (133), suggesting religious lullabies and children's prayers, and slants also the telling of "edifying stories" or the singing of hymns like "Jesus, unser Freudenmeister" during work (132). The sweetness of the *Christkind* is also mentioned in a derogatory sense (175), and "God" appears almost always with the attribute *lieb* (dear, gracious): "der liebe Gott" (201 f.), "Zwiesprache mit dem lieben Gott halten" ("to be immersed into a dialog with God gracious" — which is said of a drunken Reeperbahn innkeeper's 'gazing into the sky, 224); and "Du, die hat es doch nicht vielleicht mit dem lieben Gott?" ("Tell me, that girl isn't involved with God gracious after all, is she?" 43).

In the *Aula*, the kissing of the Bible is ridiculed (16), as is the confirmation rite (317), and there is a burlesque parody of the Lord's Supper (396 ff.; cf. also 39). The language of a theology professor and a bishop is satirically exaggerated into concentrated samples of clergy language — abundance of old-fashioned or out-dated elements, stilted and periphrastic grammar, omission of the passive auxiliary *ist* after *worden*, archaic word order, relics of Latin language, would-be-jokes etc. (25 ff. and 396 ff.). Iswall, while referring to the Lord's Supper, uses the archaic genitive object in a mocking sense: "als die anderen schon auf den Knien lagen und des heiligen Weins genossen . . .." ("when the others were already on their knees and tasting of the holy wine," 317). The same construction reoccurs in the discussion with the bishop; this time, the bishop is using it (398).

To view nature as the house of God, especially comparing a forest to a church, is a motif with a long tradition, already conventional in the works of Mörike and Eichendorff, for example; in the *Aula*, this comparison is symbolic of petty bourgeois attitude (127, 168); no less ironic is the reversal of this comparison in the fantasy about a church wedding: "Sieh mal, heute ist die Kirche wie ein Wald!" ("Just look, today the church is like a wood!" 172).

Christian prudery and ignorance of the world is another target of Kant's satire, as will become clear from the following shortened anecdote:

> Tante Mimi ist fromm, ungefähr so fromm, wie dein Hund dämlich war. Wenn die irgendwo hingen, dann nur dahin, wo der Pastor gesagt hatte, daß man da hingehen könnte . . .. Sechs Jahre sind sie verlobt gewesen und dann noch vier Jahre verheiratet, und wat nich kam, waren Kinder . . .. Der Arzt hat ihnen erklärt, ganz mit Beten allein wär die Sache nicht zu schaffen ... Kannst du dir so wat ausmalen: haben die beiden doch jahrelang auf ihrem Bettgestell gekniet und gedacht, das wäre alles! (43)

> Auntie Mimi is pious, about as pious as your dog was stupid. If she went somewhere, then it was only where the pastor had said she could go . . .. Six years they were engaged, then lived married

for another four years, and what didn't come were children . . .. The doctor explained to them that just praying wasn't enough ... Can you picture that: there had these two people been kneeling for years on their bedstead and thought that was all there was to it! (43)

A Baptist boy, a "health fanatic," is reported to have tried, with repeated reference to "Creator" and "God's handiwork," to persuade a nonsmoker to quit smoking (65). Confessionalism is exposed as well, e.g. the prejudices Catholics and Protestants have against each other (89). To make a long story short, church offices, church rites, and other things connected with religion are generally ridiculed, sometimes mildly, sometimes more sarcastically.[44]

To summarize this section: most of the religious motifs used are directed satirically against the churches, the focus being on the primitive, ritualistic, irrational, and sentimental aspects of established church traditions. Representatives of the church are to such an extent caricatures that an East German critic felt obliged to point out that the bishop was not negated in his totality.[45]

The continuous mocking use of Christian vocabulary, the more or less blasphemous use of the name of God and of religious symbols reminds one of the ridiculing of pre-Christian religions by Christianity, when, among many other things, the devil acquired his club-foot, and where other gods were changed into demons or revived for allegorical purposes, as was the *gotinne Minne* or *Vrouwe Venus* in Middle High German literature. However, Kant's criticism of religion is far from "demonizing" it; and one further function of his use of religious motifs is marxistic self-critique, criticism of certain aspects of socialism, as the following section will show.

Criticism of dogmatic phenomena in socialism

Polemics against church and against any conservative or reactionary attitude are quite usual in East German literature, as are straightforward and optimistic praises of the "progressive forces." After what has been said about the way Kant criticizes reactionary attitude, we might expect that his appraisal of his country's new order would also be humorous, and even to some extent critical. Both assumptions are indeed true and

63

can be verified through a further analysis of religious terminology, as used by Kant.

For western philosophers and publicists, it is by now commonplace to regard communism as some kind of secularized religion, as a chiliastic creed with prophetic features, as well as other attributes of western religions. In the countries of the communist block, however, these thoughts are anathema, that is, a marxist who draws such parallels for a more general critical purpose is banned as a "revisionist," "utopian liberalist," "anarchist," or whatever term seems appropriate at the moment to denounce the counter-revolutionary act of weakening Party discipline by questioning the ideological foundations of marxism or its revolutionary practice.

Kant develops the caricature of the theology professor mentioned above in a conversation between this professor and Iswall, who has gotten lost in the university building and thus come into the theologian's seminar on the Minor Prophets. Among other things, the professor says in his mocking, old-fashioned style: "Also, mein Lieber, ... nun wollen wir Ihren Schritt nicht länger bremsen, der just ansetzt zum Marsche auf die Fakultät nicht der kleinen, sondern der großen Propheten, die da Marx und Lenin geheißen . . .. " ("Well, my dear friend ... now we do not want to delay your steps any longer — steps which are just commencing to march not on the department of the Minor, but the Major Prophets, who were called Marx and Lenin ...," 27 f.). This pun is carefully prepared by mentioning the Minor Prophets two times; and there is a later reference to them, directed more to the reader than to the person addressed in the situation (36 f.).

Calling Marx and Lenin the "Major Prophets" implies criticism of dogmatic aspects of socialism, especially since this is not an isolated case in the *Aula* and since Kant inserts in this same conversation a critical allusion to East Germany's rearmament:

"Wenn also nicht zu den kleinen Propheten, wohin zieht es Sie dann, mein Freund? Zu den Feuerwerkern vielleicht, den Ballistikern und Bombardierern? Ihre Montur deutet darauf hin, aber ich fürchte, der kriegerischen Wissenschaften hat es vorerst nicht in diesem Hause, denn Gott hat es gefallen, dieses Land befreien zu lassen, und da darf so manches nicht sein." (26 f.).

"If you are not enticed by the Minor Prophets, as I see, where, then, are you bound? Perhaps to the fireworkers, the specialists in ballistics and bombardment? Your vestment, at any rate, seems to point in this direction, but I am afraid one shall not see any of the warring sciences in these halls for some time to come, for it pleased God to have this country liberated, and thusly, many a thing is not allowed to be." (27 f.)

Here, the liberation of East Germany by the Red Army is seen as an act of God; this pronouncement by a theologian is ambivalently ironic and serves as an artistic excuse for Kant's criticism of the fast rearmament of the GDR.

There is another point to be made: it is not plausible that a theologian should tamper with the principles of his own belief, as he does in this case and as is apparent also in the following quote: "Und unser aller Herr, dessen Lehre zu verbreiten wir uns hier präparieren, war eines Zimmermannes Kind. Am Ende sind Sie auch eines Zimmermannes Kind?" ("And the Lord of us all, whose teachings to spread we are here preparing ourselves, was a carpenter's son. Should you in the end be a carpenter's son, too?" 27). The artificiality of the theologian's ironies lays more responsibility for its implications on the author Kant.

Through another bourgeois character, this time a cultivated Hamburg merchant, Kant sketches rather disrespectfully the picture of communist journalists of the early fifties ("kein Gott, kein Kaiser noch Tribun und ähnlicher Klimbim"; "Sie kommen nicht hierher, um meine Seele zu retten, Sie wollen keinen Proselyten aus mir machen, ..." — "no God, or emperor, or tribune, or other knick-knack like that"; "you are not coming here in order to save my soul, you do not want to make a proselyte out of me," 137). And cancelling their nominal church membership, the young communists declare: "um gleichzeitig in der Partei und in der Kirche zu sein, dazu sind wir nicht gebildet genug. Wir sind froh, wenn wir den einen Text behalten." ("To be both in the Party and in the Church, for that we are not educated enough. We are happy if we can remember the one text." 399).

Paralleling *Doktor Martin Luther*, Kant says of *Doktor Völschow*, that his welcome speech was a preaching from the pulpit ("was der Doktor Völschow ihnen von der Kanzel gepredigt hatte . . .," 70). This man, a dogmatic, but enthusiastic stalinist, is more mildly criticized throughout;

65

behind his fight against "superstition" (*Aberglauben*, 70), idealism and true concern for his students is acknowledged.

There is another stalinist teacher who lacks the redeeming grace of idealism and only thinks in "political categories" (160). Religious metaphors are used to criticize him sarcastically as a sinister dogmatic: he seems to assume the role of "public conscience" only very reluctantly, enumerates the "sins" of the others, and convicts them of their offenses by quoting the "scriptures" (147). Angelhoff's playing "public conscience" is a satire of the practice of critique and self-critique, exposing it as a pseudo-religious ritual. There is additional irony in his self-critical reference to his "kleinbürgerliche Skrupel" (petty bourgeois scruples), since he is indeed still to a large extent a "Kleinbürger" and is said to be later purged from the Party (431).

In all of the above examples, Kant uses religious motifs as a vehicle, or at least a starting point, for his criticism of "dogmatic phenomena" in his country. The term *dogmatische Phänomene* is used indeed in connection with the student demonstration for re-naming the "Pommernplatz" (280); and Iswall's stepfather is called a "poor dogmatic" (354). In communist jargon, "dogmatism" means uncritical, mechanical application of marxistic theories or specific Party decrees. Taking this definition, it does not sound convincing if some East German critics reject emphatically the idea that the *Aula* could be a settlement with dogmatism: "Die Aula ist keine Abrechnung mit irgend einem imaginären Dogmatismus, sondern ein künstlerisches Werk dialektisch verstandener Geschichte unserer Zeit und Gesellschaft." ("The *Aula* is no settlement with some type of imaginary dogmatism, but an artistic work of dialectically conceived history of our time and society"[46]). Could it be that the *Aula* is both a settlement with a very real dogmatism, and a novel dealing with history in a dialectic manner? At any rate, the above quote illustrates the situation of East German literature — which is a bone of contention between communists and anti-communists.

Throughout the *Aula*, one finds slants against practices in socialism that resemble negative features of religion. Taking the example of doctors, Kant attacks irrational belief in science and technology:

> Mir geht der Medizinmannrummel auf die Nerven. Es steckt etwas dahinter, was mir unheimlich ist. Ich sage euch, da ist noch Mittelalter im Spiel, Herr über Tod und Leben, Ritter gegen Tod und Teufel,

Handauflegen und Besprechen, Rettung und Erlösung . . .. Sei ein Kind
vor deinem Arzt, dann wird er dir auch helfen! Glaube an ihn!
Gesundung ist Vertrauenssache! (359 f.)

That medicine-man hubbub gets on my nerves. Something's behind
it that's eerie to me. I tell you, there is still something of the Middle
Ages in it: lord of death and life, knight against death and devil,
laying on of hands and putting spells on, salvation and redemption . . ..
Be a child before your doctor, then he shall help you! Believe in
him! Recovery is a thing of trust! (359 f.)

(Compare also *Wundertiere* and *Wunder*, 360.) After Kant has derided this
irrationalism, he softens the criticism: "Aber im Ernst, das alles ist ja
nicht so wichtig" ("But in all earnestness, all of that is indeed not so
important," 360), but returns to his train of thought and imagery again
with " . . . von mir aus soll er einen hypnotischen Blick haben und
Räucherkerzen schwingen" (". . . for all I care, he can have a hypnotical
look and can wave incense around," 360 f.).

In the following, I enumerate still other slants against "dogmatic
phenomena": Kant has only a sneer for "Nachbeter" — blind adherents
— to socialist principles (388); he scorns the quoting of authorities; his
references to Stalin are full of irony and sarcasm;[47] the chanting of the
"Internationale" against a catholic service is deservedly laughed at (108).
And socialist doctrines are often treated with humor: the popular contrast
between *glauben* (to believe) and *wissen* (to know) is mocked by Grieper's
contrasting the two (221); a psychiatrist reads Engels for the sake of the
humor in it: ". . . Der klassische Weg zum Marxismus ist das wohl nicht,
aber nu, er ist Psychiater." (". . . That may not be the classical way to
marxism, but then, he's a psychiatrist." 396).

At this point, I would again like to take up Iswall's reflexions on
betraying Trullesand. In this long passage, the devil metaphor is important
not only stylistically, but even more so thematically. Kant pretends to
expect a little imagination from the reader in using the devil as an image
("aber ein wenig Phantasie muß ich schon verlangen können," 432); but
what he actually does is disappoint the expectations of Socialist Realism.
Consequently, Kant was charged with practically wasting his reflexions
about the devil's function and character in the transition period where
socialism was being built up.[48] This criticism was directed against Kant's

staying with the poetic mystification. The metaphor of the devil suggests indeed a more pervasive and lasting principle than just temporary difficulties resulting from non-antagonistic contradictions. Moreover, while refusing to resolve the devil metaphor, Kant ridicules the usual textbook solution to the problem of good and evil, accident and necessity, cause and effect, by imagining that the dogmatic Angelhoff explains

> daß der Teufel nur eines der vielen Synonyme des Zufalls sei und der Zufall nur der Schnittpunkt jener Striche, die Vernunft und Unvernunft durch die Geschichte ziehen . . .. Überdies hätte er in diesem Falle auch nicht helfen können mit seinen Kausallinien, denn wo ist der gesetzmäßige Zusammenhang zwischen drei Jahren Freundschaft und einem fast tödlichen Krach am letzten Tage. (431)

> that the devil was only one of the many synonyms of accident, and accident only the intersection of those lines that are drawn through history by reason and unreason . . .. Besides, he couldn't have helped in this case with his causal lines, for where is the rule-governed connection between three years of friendship and an almost deadly quarrel on the last day. (431)

There is another place in the *Aula* where Kant speaks critically of the usual explanation of accident as being the intersection of two necessities (99). This simple textbook explanation of the problem accident-necessity was indeed challenged — and still is — by marxistic philosophers, in particular by the East German scientist and philosopher Robert Havemann. He claimed that dialectical marxism was being reduced to a simplistic determinism of the Laplace type; based on recent scientific discoveries, he proposed that one "cause" can have different consequences.[49]

When Iswall "returns the borrowed devil" (433), he hints at misuse of Party power and bureaucracy behind the facade of an open talk between comrades: he does not want to talk about the excuses and scruples of his friend, one reads; but one is told that the discussion lasts for three hours. The result of that meeting is that two people who have never even thought of marrying or going to Peking do marry and do go to Peking for seven years — a result that everyone present at that meeting contributed to. One of the participants, another student, receives perhaps an even worse Party task than the seven years in Peking. At any rate, there is some connection between this meeting and his going to Hamburg; and this mission or escape to Hamburg is referred to as a "bad miracle" ("ein böses Wunder," 187). This is not the whole story, however: as usual, Kant has a complex motivation. The pivotal point for the whole story is Iswall's "treacherous" suggestion; and the reasons for this suggestion seem to be that the irrational forces in the individual and in society may at times be stronger than the principles of socialism allow.

What Kant rejects in the end with the unresolved devil metaphor is an oversimplified view of man. In another scene, Iswall summarizes his experience with a girlfriend whom he could not convince of his own socialistic ideas, and tries to give his friend a piece of advice in sermonizing form in case he should ever get into a similar situation:

> . . . dann denke nicht, [. . .] daß die Umwelt den Menschen verändert und das Sein das Bewußtsein und daß das Neue unaufhaltsam ist und du bist das Neue und du wirst schon auf sie abfärben . . .. Stehe auf und renne, ... Amen. (128)

> . . . then don't think [. . .] that the environment changes man, and existence, consciousness, and that the new is irresistible, and that you are the new and will get around to it as time goes by, ... Arise and run, ... Amen. (128)

Again and again, Kant ridicules the official East German doctrine about the new man, especially in application to literature. Direktor Meibaum and his views are ironized: " [. . .] die neue Literatur, die muß doch optimistisch sein, das ergibt sich aus unserer Gesellschaftsordnung; das ist, möchte ich sagen, gesetzmäßig" — (" [. . .] the new literature, it has to be optimistic, doesn't it; that's simply the consequence of our new social order; that is, I would say, necessarily so" 266). The very title of a socialist *Moraltute* (Morals trumpet), namely "Du sollst nicht stehlen!" (*Thou Shalt Not Steal!*, 33) is ironic, and Kant chastises the shallow optimism of this type of literature by the ironic suggestion to call a book about sugar theft in the post-war times "Du sollt nicht begehren des anderen Zucker" (*Thou Shalt Not Covet Thy Neighbor's Sugar*, 265). Using the formula of the Ten Commandments, Kant suggests that this type of socialistic morality is merely watered-down Christian morality, and no less hypocritical.

In the above imagined booktitle there may also be a satirical slant against the "Ten Commandments of Socialistic Morality" as proclaimed by Walter Ulbricht in 1958. These Commandments contain the following precepts: "Thou shalt perform good deeds for Socialism because Socialism leads to a better life for all workers. Thou shalt strive to increase thine output ... Thou shalt lead a clean, decent life and respect thy family ...."[50] Another reference to these Commandments in the *Aula* is connected with Jakob Filter: in a fictive part of Iswall's Aula speech, he is called upon to perform "good deeds" ("gute Taten") as a way of returning the investment put into his education by state and society (367). (Incidentally, East German college students are indeed expected to feel grateful and obliged to the taxpayer for their college education.)

Kant prefers an independent, curious mind to doctrinaire blindfolds (187); he pleads for overcoming fanaticism and mistrust (162), and he proposes to face the enemy within one's self rather than project one's conflicts on a scapegoat or "enemy" (160 ff., 407). Again, Kant rarely has his hero Iswall express this creed directly; it is usually veiled. One of the disguises is Iswall's self-stylization as a preacher.[51] His first girlfriend Inga, a preacher's daughter, discovers the "sermonizing style" in his ideological talk:

> — eine Predigt hast du gehalten, darauf verstehe ich mich. Und so etwas nennt sich ungläubig ... und hält eine Predigt, daß man kein Sünder mehr sein möchte, sondern ein Engel seinetwegen, ein Deutscher Demokratischer Engel. Setz dich auf dein Fahrrad, du Prediger, dein Himmel wartet — und meine Mutter auch. (106)

> — what you did was preach a sermon, I know about those things. And a guy like that calls himself unbelieving ... and he delivers a sermon that one would not like to be a sinner any longer, but an angel on account of his preaching, a German Democratic Angel. Get on your bicycle, you preacher, your heaven is waiting — and so is my mother. (106)

Here, the ironic form does not destroy the seriousness of Kant-Iswall's deepest convictions; and in a later passage toward the end of the book (and of the plot), where Iswall has a hilarious prayer meditation about private and public problems, the concluding petition for peace is quite serious (417 f.).

Further considerations

I would like to add several further remarks about the validity and the range of this analysis of religious language and motifs. First, it is not always indicated who is using religious language, nor are the characters using religious terms described in any detail. If one were to add this background information, one would get further results; yet these refinements of interpretation would not affect the substance of the findings here, but rather would provide richer nuances of what has been termed "dialectical humor."

As far as the field of religious motifs is concerned, the question may arise why one should not include parallels between elements of the novel and corresponding elements of religion, and whether there is not more systematic religious symbolism used than the various main "functions" sketched in this analysis. The crucial point here is to define what exactly is meant by "corresponding elements"; this definition would presuppose certain assumptions, which would burden a literary analysis and which would, in the final analysis, subject the interpretation to arbitrariness. It is possible to apply the archetypal pattern of paradise-fall-redemption to Iswall's life (including repentance and confession) — but does the novel itself suggest to do this? Again, one might see Christ images in reference to Iswall or Trullesand: Trullesand, for one thing, happens to be a carpenter; and this fact makes him use the "Zimmermann Joseph" (Carpenter Joseph) in discussions about the importance of carpentry, and makes him point to the fact that "Jesus von Nazareth einen Zimmermann zum Vater gehabt habe," ("Jesus of Nazareth had a carpenter for a father," 51). In Iswall's comment on this, he says that Trullesand's later profession had nothing to do with the "Jesusvater" ("Jesus' father"), but asserts, in a somewhat obscure way, that there may be a connection between "biblical times" and Trullesand's studying Chinese literature for seven years (51 f.). Iswall himself is asked in one scene if he is by any chance "a carpenter's son" (27). On the other hand, Iswall could be compared to Judas Ischarioth or Peter since there is a betrayal scene, the words reminding somewhat of Isaiah 53:3 (315); and Trullesand's fishing during the confession scene could be interpreted as a playful counterfeiture of New Testament accounts of fishing; similarly, one could parallel Trullesand's hilarious "teachings" to Christ's teachings, and point to the fact that his black curly hair is frequently mentioned: at this point at the latest it becomes clear that such an extension of the definition of "religious motifs" would necessarily lead into speculations that are only based on intuition. It is a more promising task to investigate which place Kant holds in respect to his obvious use of religious language in the century-long process of secularization of the Christian religion. The fact that the *Aula* is so clearly part of this secularization process suggests that this author — and perhaps socialist literature as a whole — is actually closely linked to Western literary traditions; and that the "revolutionary socialist literature" may be, in a sense, more conservative than the avant-garde literature of "decadent bourgeois culture."

A comparison of Kant's use of religious language and religious motifs with other authors goes well beyond the objective of this study. There was, in pre-marxist socialism, a strand of Christian socialism, at least of socialists who used all elements of Christian religion to preach their new gospel; the best example is perhaps Wilhelm Weitling in his book "Das Evangelium eines armen Sünders" (*The Gospel of a Poor Sinner*). In this book, which appeared in 1845 and had a wide appeal, Weitling preached in prophetic language his gospel of revolution, and called for "a Messiah to lead the workers to a society of equals governed by scientists and sages . . .. Jesus was a communist and primitive Christianity a shining example of equality and brotherhood."[52]

The above book appeared more than a hundred years ago, but there are still literary traditions which use biblical language and concepts for strong emphasis in an affirmative sense. Johannes R. Becher, with his expressionistic and neo-classicist style, is the most important and influential model. The style of Johannes R. Becher includes, together with other expressionistic and neo-classicist features, ample use of religious imagery. He used this religious language as a means of describing his vision of communism, and, more concretely, to praise Stalin and Ulbricht. Kant rarely, if ever, uses religious language in this affirmative sense; his generally ironic use of religious language may actually imply that he scorns the style and the literary traditions of Becher and his disciples.

During the student demonstration, Kant has two students discuss once more the controversial question of whether the Bible is a requirement for a person's general education ("ob die Bibel zur Allgemeinbildung gehöre," 291). Again, no agreement is reached; and Kant himself does not give any direct answer to this question. Yet, as seen throughout the *Aula*, the Bible and its language remain very much a part of the developing socialist culture.

Types and Functions of Imagery

The Schlenstedts note, with an indication of disapproval, that there are almost no symbolic metaphors in Kant's *Aula*.[53] Indeed, Kant usually avoids obvious symbols, and if he does use conventional imagery, he does it tongue-in-cheek. Kant is, in Schiller's terms, a sentimental author; his imagery is rarely taken from nature, but instead much more frequently from culture — from man's social world. Kant's imagery is intellectual rather than atmospheric; he prefers metaphors which are in some respect inadequate, paradoxical, ironical, and satirical; in short, what has been called "dialectical humor" is constitutive for Kant's imagery, as well.

As for the imagery of landscape and the elemental natural forces, it is interesting to observe that Kant uses those few metaphors and similes mainly in connection with problematic relationships of Iswall to other persons. In the case of Iswall's fragile friendship or love for Inga, one finds an unfolding of the ice-plate simile (125 ff.). With Iswall's second love relationship, the reader can enjoy a veritable fireworks of playfully entwined metaphors based on the two equations of love to wine and love to fire: in this case, there is no clash in basic convictions and beliefs between Iswall and his girlfriend; the only possible danger lies in Iswall himself, in the part he refers to as "Innen-Iswall" (413 f.). In both cases, there is an element of parody and self-irony present that destroys any mystification or romantic atmosphere.

Kant's nature imagery is conventional and/or derived from idiomatic expressions. And yet, despite all anti-romantic turns, and despite all humorous disillusionments of the traditional concept that love is an elemental force, there remains a strong suggestion: namely, that man's emotions and passions are neither readily explainable nor easily changeable or controllable.

Kant seems to shun metaphors from the fields of science, technology, and economics — fields strongly represented in the works of many of his colleagues; likewise, he avoids personification of technical or economic objects. Although Iswall — and Kant himself in real life — were electrical craftsmen, Kant does not take much advantage of his chance to show a connection between this area of material production and intellectual superstructure; however, there are occasional jokes like "weil ich bei Schika durchhing wie ein Zinkkabel im Sommer," ("since I sagged in Schika's class like a zinc cable in summer," 424).

The rare personifications, e. g. a disease "giggling" and "rubbing its hands with glee" etc. (149) are humorous, too, as well as the frequent cases of animal imagery already discussed in connection with elements of popular or colloquial style.[54] To call Grieper's memories "Erinnerungen einer fett und lahm gewordenen Kanalratte" ("memories of a gutter rat grown fat and lame," 94), means to use a down-to-earth, effective metaphor, in this case for the sake of ideological polemics; the combination "fat and lame" adds to these polemics a flair of rhetorical refinement.

Imagery of aggression

There is some sports imagery in the *Aula*, like the boxing terms "Treffer landen" and "nach Punkten vorn liegen" (to score a hit; to be leading in points, 201), and the ski terms *Slalom* and *Schußfahrt* (403). Like animal imagery, these expressions, too, belong to popular, colloquial style. Sports imagery is part of the imagery of aggression, in so far as sports are ritualized aggression. Other segments of the field of aggression, more specifically, the imagery of war and fighting, give the most interesting examples of figurative speech in the *Aula*, second only perhaps to the imagery of religion.

It is at first surprizing that this novel, written from the perspective of the "un-warlike" Iswall should contain as many and as prominent figures of speech using motifs of aggression as it does. Early in the book, Kant introduces the rhetorical paradox that Iswall, who was "as non-belligerent as onyone could be," yet lived "through a thousand battles," and was "lifted on the shield" in the Aula as valedictorian (11). There is also the rather strong statement, directed against any force or violence: "Gewalt ist fast immer idiotisch, und ebensooft ist sie die Folge von Angst" ("Force is almost always idiotic, and, just as often, it is the result of fear," 419).

It should be added that East German military forces are nowhere praised; in the few references to them, there is always a critical tone perceivable (286, 369; see also 232, probably a slant against the "Gesellschaft für Sport und Technik," East Germany's paramilitary youth organization).

Since Iswall is described as opposed to violence, it is interesting to consider which use he makes of imagery of aggression in his reflections, and with which persons he associates this kind of language.

The director of the "Workers' and Peasants' College," Dr. Mevius Völschow, uses the expression "die Feste Wissenschaft stürmen" (to storm the fortress of science) so frequently that it must be called a leitmotif. One should remember that the phrase "Stürmt die Feste Wissenschaft!" was the official motto of the "educational revolution" in East Germany after the War, a process often referred to by Western authors as bolshevization of science and education. A similar phrase was used in 1959 by Walter Ulbricht to describe the goal of the "Bitterfeld Movement," namely "die Höhen der Kultur stürmen" ("to storm the summits of culture").[55] As already noted, the figure of Völschow is a mixed one; he possesses idealistic verve and inspiring enthusiasm, but, on the other hand, proves to be a stalinist. Thus, the leitmotivic emphasis on the motto "Storm the fortress of science!" combines acknowledgment of positive changes in the educational field with criticism of the force and violence used in that process.[56]

Iswall's and Trullesand's entering the campus of their college for the first time is compared to the "Sturm auf das Winterpalais" ("the storming of the Winter Palace"), one of the classical episodes of the Russian October Revolution (10). This comparison is a humorous variation of — or, in the sequence of the plot, an anticipation of — the motif "Stürmt die Feste Wissenschaft!" Iswall allows himself to extend the comparison with the Winter Palace episode into some detail, but retracts it immediately as indulgence in "romanticism." Yet the same comparison is taken up later on in the novel again, and is contrasted with another variation of the storm-attack motif; this time, Trullesand's stay in China is metaphorically called the conquest of a remote outpost ("ein abgelegenes Außenfort [. . .] erobern," 304 f; cf. also 371). Despite the obvious humor, there is a note of disappointment in this passage, as in the other references to Trullesand's stay in Peking.

The figure of Völschow is more than only a humorous caricature of a benevolent stalinist; and the motto of the socialistic educational revolution is subtly connected with certain German traditions. Völschow receives the nickname "Alter Fritz," the popular name for the legendary King Frederick the Great of Prussia, because of his physiognomy (28, 40,

372). Völschow is indeed heir to the Prussian tradition in many ways. Two other leitmotifs in Völschow's speech must be mentioned in this connection; the first is the quotation "Des Geistes Licht, des Wissens Macht, dem ganzen Volke sei's gegeben!" ("Enlightenment of Mind, and Power of Knowledge, may they be given to all the people!", 70). The other is a quote from the same poem:

> Wir sind nicht reif!
> Das ist das Lied, das sie gesungen haben
> jahrhundertelang uns armen Waisenknaben. (70)

> We are not mature enough!
> That is the tune they have been chanting
> For centuries to us poor orphans. (70)[57]

The three motifs of storm attack, claim to enlightenment, and suppression of "orphans" are introduced together in Völschow's welcoming speech to the new proletarian students, more specifically, these three motifs summarize his speech (70); and it may be more than a coincidence that these motifs again occur in Völschow's talk during the Party meeting which resulted in Trullesand's going to Peking (434; cf. also 306 and 311). The phrase "to let an endless line of suppressed and unrecognized orphans march up" appears to be particularly important, combining the orphan motif with the motif of military attack (434).

The above poem quotes resound the ideals of democracy, idealistic philosophy, enlightenment, and, in the last analysis, Christian traditions, all of which are parts of the Prussian heritage. But "Preußentum" is mainly notorious for its militarism; and it is my interpretation that Kant suggests in the figure of Völschow a continuation of both the idealistic and the militaristic traditions of old Prussia in East Germany's cultural revolution.

Kant's view of East Germany's cultural revolution is also visible in the following scene, where again war imagery is used. In a student meeting where candidates for student representation are to be voted on, the proletarian students have at first a difficult stand against the reactionary majority (206 ff.). A candidate of theirs is admitted only after he delivers an impressive speech which is largely an imitation ot the famous Nicias speech from the *Peloponnesian War* by Thucydides (216 ff.). In this long speech, East Germany's social changes towards Socialism are compared to a campaign — of which the student election constitutes one single battle — in which a "victory" should be won for "reason." We have here a perfect example of ironically balanced and humorously softened affirmation of the basic marxistic idea of class-struggle.

War imagery, as used by the teacher Angelhoff, betrays the attitude of militant suspicion and fanatic intolerance, as when this teacher sees an "attack of the class-enemy" in a physician's concern for a student who has a mild case of tuberculosis (158 ff.):

Die Frage ist eine politische. Wir befinden uns hier in einer ehemaligen Kaserne, einem von uns eroberten Raubnest des deutschen Militarismus. Der Feind ist geschlagen, aber ist er schon vernichtet? Nein. Es kommt jedoch darauf an, ihn zu vernichten. Aber was sehen wir, wenn wir hier hinausblicken? Wir sehen uns fast eingeschlossen von einer Obstbaumsiedlung, von Laubenkolonien, Schrebergärten, von kleinbürgerlichem Besitz. Wie aber ist der Kleinbürger, Genosse Trullesand? [...] Richtig, die Kleinbürger schwanken. Sie schwanken auch jetzt. Sie haben sich noch nicht entschieden. Sie sind bereit, mit dem Stärkeren zu gehen. Wir sind die Stärkeren, das wissen sie, und darum beginnen sie, sich auf uns zu orientieren, aber bei dem geringsten Zeichen von Schwäche in unseren Reihen werden sie sich wieder abwenden — eine einzige weiche Stelle würde ihnen genügen... (158 ff.)

The question is a political one. We find ourselves here in a former baracks, in a robbers' den of German militarism conquered by us. The enemy is defeated, but is he already destroyed? No. What matters, however, is to destroy him. But what do we see, when we look out here? We see ourselves almost entirely encircled by plots of fruit-trees, by cottage settlements, by Schreber gardens, by petty bourgeois property. But what is the petty bourgeois like, Comrade Trullesand? [...] Right, the petty bourgeois waver. They are wavering also now. They have not yet made their choice. They are ready to go with the stronger. We are the stronger ones, they know that, and therefore they begin to look to us for leadership; but at the slightest sign of weakness in our ranks, they will again turn away — a single soft spot would suffice them... (158 ff.)

The immanent satire here is evident: Angelhoff blows up the "soft spot" of the student's tuberculosis into a breakthrough of the "class enemy," and the pseudo-logic of his inferences, the ridiculous symbolism of baracks and orchards, and the excessive use of military imagery in this specific situation are truly "self-defeating." The imagery used here is derived from the central marxistic idea of class-struggle, which leads to formations like *der Klassenfeind*, or simply *der Gegner* (160 f.).

The scene quoted above calls for a discussion of the term *Wachsamkeit* (vigilance), and this term deserves special attention (40, 148 f.). *Wachsamkeit* was the official watchword of the times, given out as a motto for vigilance in ideological matters and for fighting anti-Soviet tendencies: in May 1949, the SED board (Parteivorstand) criticized "Erscheinungen mangelnder Wachsamkeit in ideologischen Fragen und von Duldsamkeit gegenüber antisowjetischen Stimmungen" ("Instances of insufficient vigilance in ideological matters and of toleration of anti-Soviet tendencies"); the resolution of this conference became a euphemism for rigorous suppression of ideas deviating in any direction from the official, Soviet-guided Party-line.

Kant does not criticize the above aspect of East Germany's post-war situation directly or generally, but deals in some detail with one single case of misdirected "vigilance," indicating however widespread confusion of vigilance and self-defeating suspicion. Kant gives a clear hint as to how extensive the misuse of the motto of "Wachsamkeit" was: Party Secretary Haiduck has his secretary write a letter to Angelhoff in which he explains to him the real meaning of the term; and his secretary comments that she has already written "dozens of such letters" (163).

After a classroom discussion of Keller's "Abendlied," the proponent of Keller's atheism is described as *wachsam-zufrieden* (114). Here, "vigilance" is alluded to in a rather humorous manner, but with clear reference to "ideological questions" raised and fought over in that discussion; as a matter of fact, the discussion is likened at two places to a military action, through the metaphorical use of "wall" and "rampart" — an example of "class-war" in the "class-room," with all its comical and serious implications.

Party Secretary Haiduck, a veteran of the Spanish Civil War, is entitled to use war imagery without being ironized. It is he who explains the difference between "vigilance" and "suspicion" in the above mentioned letter; and this letter closes with the lines:

Wachsamkeit hat mit Mut zu tun. Mißtrauen hat mit Angst zu tun. Mißtrauen schießt auf Gespenster. Das ist Munitionsvergeudung, und die ist strafbar. (163)

Vigilance has to do with courage. Mistrust has to do with fear. Mistrust shoots at ghosts. That is a waste of ammunition, and that is punishable. (163)

The importance of this letter is emphasized not only by mentioning that it has been written dozens of times, but also by its connection to Haiduck's service in the Civil War; the above section of the letter is said to be something like a legacy in that it uses an order of the day issued to his brigade (164).

Angelhoff's "class enemy" (or his "agent"), Dr. Gropjuhn, also uses military imagery, more specifically expressions taken from the officers' jargon — but he does so humorously, and a bit in defiance of the opportunism around him; it is mentioned explicitly that he had not been a militarist during his career as a medical officer (162, 149 f.).

Some imagery of aggression is applied to people representing real capitalism. However, the metaphors used are conventional and moreover anachronistic: Grieper's stories are called *Räubergeschichten* (robbers' stories) and "Saga seiner dreißig Gaunerjahre" (saga of his thirty 'crooky' years, 93 f.); and his wife is said to have been sitting in the *Räubersattel* (robber's saddle) for a long time (95). Humorous as these expressions may be, they contain criticism of capitalistic exploitation and denounce the underlying economic principles as out-of-date.

Imagery of war and fighting and of other kinds of aggression is a common feature of everyday language and of literature. For the sensitive, historically minded person, words like *kämpferisch* (fighting) and *Kämpfer* (fighter) may be discredited for literary purposes because they still remind of how the Nazi propaganda glorified heroes like Schlageter and Wessel as being *kämpferisch*. However, in East German official usage, these words are very frequently used clichés. To give just one example in point: it is not without a certain irony that this kind of language is applied to the *Aula* itself in a booklet published by the East German "Deutsches Theater" on occasion of their production of the *Aula*'s theater version; in this little brochure, *Kampf* and *Sieg* are favorite expressions; we find *Kämpfer*, *Niederlagen*, *Widerstände*, and even the phrase "schöne, kampfreiche Zeit" (fight, victory; fighters, defeats, resistance, beautiful time of battles). [58]

It is in the context of this kind of language usage that Kant's use of imagery of aggression has to be seen and evaluated, and it seems worth-while to consider the implications.

Marxism conceives of historical events as the results of opposing forces; to use a well-known formula, "all history is a history of class struggles." However, there were, from the very beginning of marxist thought, two different views as to the nature of this changing historical scene, i.e., the concepts of evolution and of revolution. With some simplification, one can say that the young Marx, moderate marxists, and certain political movements like the European Social Democrats, have held to the evolutionary position, whereas Leninist-Stalinist and Maoist marxism take the revolutionary position, resorting to non-revolutionary initiatives (like coexistence) only for tactical purposes, and branding all evolutionary tendencies as "revisionism" or similar deviations. This holds for the theory, but it is a different question what the various socialist countries are practicing in reality, a question too lengthy to be considered here. However, it is interesting to note that the concept of "revolution" itself has become blurred, as the meanings of *Revolution, revolutionär,* and *revolutionieren* have become more and more extended, being applied to any progressive activity. An example can be found in the *Aula* itself: the peaceful, orderly demonstration for re-naming the "Pommerplatz" is called "revolutionäres Tun" and "revolutionäre Situation" (282); the speaker, it should be added, however, is the dogmatic Angelhoff.

Clearly, Kant exposes false heroism, empty propaganda, and fanatical dogmatism — but does he also criticize, in some way, revolutionary theory? It would seem that he indeed does. The strict, "classical" version of marxistic philosophy has it that aggression, in the sense of violent, destructive activity, is only a consequence of suppressive social conditions. Therefore, a fight against these conditions is believed to be justified and inevitable, and the changes in the basis are expected to be sufficient to remove radically the old antinomies, thus ending all alienation.

Incidentally, the words "aggression" and "aggressor" are used in communist jargon only with reference to military actions of "reactionary movements." If a "progressive" movement should attack, it would be called "liberation"; but then, the Romans did not conquer other nations either, but "brought peace" to them.

80

Kant seems to suggest a more objective, differentiated view of the problem of aggression; the imagery of aggression, together with the other motifs of violence and destruction he uses in the *Aula*, point in the direction of the following thoughts: economics may not be the only reason for aggression; even "constructive aggression," that is, revolutionary violence, may vitiate the cause of communism; and revolutionary ardor for a good cause may be combined with the projection of unresolved conflicts onto a "scapegoat" enemy. For himself, Iswall states that "the real name of the enemy was always Robert Iswall" ("... mit seinem wahren Namen hieß er [der Gegner, T. L.] immer nur Robert Iswall," 407). In the situation, this refers to "villains" which Iswall's cowardice puts between himself and an embarrassing confrontation, as he sees it himself; however, this statement has a much wider application.

In this connection, Iswall's reflexions on the term *Meinungsstreit* are very interesting (35). The expression "struggle of opinions" — referring to a milder variant of disagreement in place of the former critique and self-critique — prompts Iswall to muse about the relation between word and thing: "[...] es geht ja nicht um das Wort, sondern um die Sache, um die Haltung, die man zu einer Meinung einnimmt" (35). Iswall acknowledges here the limitations of words; what really matters, he says, is the thing itself, in this case the attitude one takes towards an opinion. This is a criticism of the former ritual of critique and self-critique; the authority of a dogma, and the ruthless battling-down of opinions disagreeing with the official Party line, is being replaced by a form of struggle in which arguments have to be "taken serious" — unless *Meinungsstreit* is just another euphemism for the old enforcement of discipline. Beyond this, Kant seems to regret that in his society the non-violent way of arriving at an agreement is not yet the only one. Kant closes these reflections with Iswall's intention to show in his speech "how they had had to learn everything anew, also the art of treating each other reasonably" ("auch die Kunst, vernünftig miteinander umzugehen," 35).

At this point, it may be added that Kant does acknowledge other aspects of changing social relationships; we do find imagery and other motifs from areas like education, growth, development, improvement, design, construction, and cooperation. However, considering the prominence of imagery of aggression, it seemed justified to concentrate mainly on this area.

The preceding interpretation leading to the inference that Kant does indeed modify some points of revolutionary theory and practice will not be generally accepted. More agreement may be reached for the conclusion that Kant is a critic of revolutionary attire in a post-revolutionary or pseudo-revolutionary situation, assuming that a definition of revolution is agreed upon. There will be general agreement, however, that Kant's aesthetic position is a further development of early socialistic positions. The East German literature immediately after the War is frequently called "antifascist-democratic"; literature was regarded as a tool of revolution and a "weapon against decadence and formalistic perversions," with the expressionistic slogan "Kunst ist Waffe" (Art is a weapon) being adapted to the specific situation of East Germany.[59] Kant's position is that of critical pro-socialism; his motto could well be "Art must be more than a weapon."

Technique and Functions of Literary References

Socialist literature

The *Aula* contains a host of quotations, allusions, and other references to the literary world. An analysis of these references will contribute to a description of Kant's style and literary technique; furthermore, such an analysis promises to delineate Kant's own position within the literary tradition. For this second purpose, several points of the introduction must be elaborated upon.

First, the historical dimension of the East German literary scene must be outlined; present-day socialist positions in the area of culture cannot be properly understood without some knowledge of past issues and developments within the communist movement.

In the development of a communist theory of the arts, after the Russian October Revolution, two rivalling tendencies clashed openly. To the "left" were the proponents of "Proletkult." They held that with a new social order a radically new, anti-traditional, proletarian art had to be created. The "right wing" position was that the positive, progressive aspects of all art had always been realistic, and that Socialist Realism was the fulfilment rather than the "undialectical" replacement of previous art forms.

Lenin turned against the "Proletkult" as early as 1919. Lenin's less radical position has remained victorious till this day in the Soviet-led socialist countries. Since then, a key term has been the word "Erbe" (heritage); this concept implies that there are certain cultural products created by the progressive artists of the times, and that these lasting treasures belong to all mankind and can only be received, guarded, and creatively re-assimilated by the emerging socialist societies. This meant that socialism claimed, e. g., the Weimar classics as theirs, and denied the legitimacy of the National Socialist claim to fulfill the legacy of Hölderlin.[60] In practice, however, this "positive reception of the heritage" was always in danger of leading to sterile imitation, as the example of Becher proves.

Whereas the East German literary establishment typically simplifies literary questions, Kant emphasizes the complexitiy of cultural phenomena: he does lay claim on the classical traditions, but warns at the same time of the dangers of mechanical "Erberezeption"; in the case of the "new type" of literature, he warns that not all that glitters with newness is really so new, and in the case of some "non-progressive" literature, he suggests that it had and still has its merits.

First, references to contemporary writers of East Germany will be dealt with. In a conversation with his former dean, Iswall mentions a young author who presented the plan for a novel for which he had already found a title: "Doch ewig bleiben die Steine" (*But Forever Remain the Stones*), a project intended to grow to nine hundred pages within two years (266). This title combines Gulbranssen's epic "Und ewig singen die Wälder" and Erik Neutsch's "Die Spur der Steine." Neutsch's book, a combination of a socialistic industrial novel and a love story, is indeed over nine hundred pages long. This novel is also satirically alluded to in Iswall's playfully suggested book title "Des Zuckers Spur" (*The Sugar's Trace*, 265) and in his reflections on "des Teufels Spur" (the devil's trace, 433).

In the same scene, Iswall speaks of an apprentice's romance with no less a title than "Das bläst der Wind nicht fort" (*This Will Not Blow with the Wind*, 266). This title is an allusion to a novel by Max Walter Schulz "Wir sind nicht Staub im Wind" (*We Are Not Dust in the Wind*). Kant adds a variation of this title: "Kein Sturm, der uns die Träume nimmt" (*No Storm to Take Our Dreams*, 266), perhaps an allusion to Arnold Zweig's 1962 novel "Traum ist teuer."

What is Kant criticizing with titles like "Das bläst der Wind nicht fort," and "Doch ewig bleiben die Steine"? In the scene in which these titles are mentioned, Direktor Meibaum and Iswall are discussing the speech Iswall is supposed to deliver at the upcoming celebration, and Iswall intersperses several satirical comments about his East German colleagues. Here Iswall explicitly criticizes the "thick books" ("ganz dicke Bücher") which are going to be fashionable again; these books have presumptuous titles and are programmatically directed against Mitchell's *Gone with the Wind*, often using the same area of imagery.

In Schulz's novel itself, one finds the quote from Immermann's *Epigonen* "Was bläst denn unser Leben — die vielen Leben — zusammen und wieder auseinander?" ("What is it that blows our life — the many lives — together and again apart?").[61] This question is a leitmotif in Immermann's novel and expresses the feeling of being doomed to be only "Epigonen," weighted down by the great achievements of the past, powerless and impotent, unable to create anything genuinely new and lasting. Schulz's use of this motif is directed against this fatalistic resignation and proposes, instead, an optimistic, action-oriented outlook: he gives his 1962 novel the presumptuous subtitle "Roman einer unverlorenen Generation ("Novel of an Un-lost Generation").[62]

Iswall's dialog partner cannot quite follow, but senses there is something wrong in the way Iswall criticizes the "new literature":

Ich weiß nicht, Genosse Iswall, ich glaube, deine Auffassung ist nicht völlig richtig; die neue Literatur, die muß doch optimistisch sein, das ergibt sich doch aus unserer neuen Gesellschaftsordnung; das ist, möchte ich sagen, gesetzmäßig. (266)

I don't know, Comrade Iswall, but I believe your view is not quite right; the new literature, it must be optimistic, that simply follows from our new social order; that is, I would say, necessarily so. (266)

Iswall is all too familiar with this position of non-dialectical optimism. In the course of his first meditation on possible topics for his Aula speech, he anticipates Meibaum's negative reaction to the mentioning of Mitchell's *Gone with the Wind*: Meibaum is certain to reject the very idea of mentioning his having read this "elegy on the destruction of Southern feudalism"; instead, Iswall reasons ironically, he might suggest Ilja Ehrenburg's *The*

Storm, "or something else with a progressive breeze" (16 f.; cf. also 14, 266).

Throughout the *Aula,* Iswall's critical mind challenges the dogmatic belief that everything written with a socialistic perspective is automatically a unique and lasting monument. Kant suggests that many of his colleagues are actually concocting worn clichés, using stereotype imagery, falling into hollow pathos, and pretending earthiness rather than developing the promised counter-literature to the allegedly out-dated bourgeois writings.

Trite storm imagery is also to be found, again with reference to Mitchell's epic, in Erwin Strittmatter's successful novel *Ole Bienkopp* where Mitchell's novel is adored as the "bible of the soul" by a romantic, mis-educated girl who has to live as the wife of a ranger in a little village.[63]

There are other aspects of the East German literary scene which Kant takes up in the *Aula.* As a journalist, Iswall is asked to write a review of a novella "Du sollst nicht stehlen" (*Thou Shalt Not Steal,* 33). Iswall calls this product a *Moraltute* (morals trumpet), the lady-writer's name being incidentally "Tuschmann" (literally "Fanfare-man"). What Iswall resents about this piece is its narrow-minded, quasi-religious morality, as well as its "billiard-ball" psychology, and he resents this all the more since he is expected to write a "constructive criticism" (34).

Iswall returns several times to this novella; in the scene with Direktor Meibaum, he alters the title ironically to "Du sollst nicht begehren des anderen Zucker" (*Thou Shalt Not Covet Another's Sugar*), and later to "Zucker und Hammer" (*Sugar and Hammer*) and to "Des Zuckers Spur" (*The Sugar's Trace*), a title mentioned earlier (265).

In this situation, "sugar" refers to a story of the austere post-war period in which a man steals sugar from his factory by throwing the sugar over a fence and is finally found out by a friend. In Meibaum's opinion, this negative episode could have been a positive one: the thief could not only have quit his stealing, but, pressured by his friend, he could have become a hammer thrower for the greater glory of his region and won an upcoming competition. Iswall ridicules this fantasy — at least for the reader. There may be further implications, however; for in German there is an idiomatic combination "Zuckerbrot und Peitsche" ("sugared bread and whip"), an expression for the combination of reward and punishment in training of animals, metaphorically used for conditioning of people. Also, a hammer is one of the emblems in East Germany's flag.

The heroes of this kind of literature are supposed to be examples of "high morality." As for the expected "high morality" of the person who found out how the sugar thieves operated, Kant suggests to the reader that this new morality may actually be rather questionable since it is based on suspicion and rigid enforcement of general principles, excluding personal, situational decisions.

With a title such as *Thou Shalt Not Steal*, Kant also alludes to the "Ten Commandments of Socialistic Morality" proclaimed by East German Chairman Walter Ulbricht.[64] With this allusion to biblical language, Kant seems to criticize watered-down, petty-bourgeois morality in socialistic trappings.

Another aspect of socialistic literature scorned by Kant is the panegyric tone of propaganda lyrics. Expressions like *Völkerführer* (leader of the nations), and "Sohn des Schuhmachers aus Gori" (son of the shoemaker from Gori, 281), which refer to Stalin, are reminiscent of the "cult of personality" era in East Germany and in the entire Eastern hemisphere. During this era, even respectable authors contributed their hymns, odes, or cantatas to the Stalin cult; and until this day, no full and open settlement with all aspects of this dark chapter of communistic development has been undertaken in the socialist countries.

Kant's allusions to these Stalin poems are rather indirect. The expressions just quoted are found in the fierce discussion of the dogmatic teacher Angelhoff with a student who dares as much as minimal critical, independent thinking about one specific incident of "cult of personality." Kant speaks, in connection with this scene, of "dogmatic phenomena" (280); and he makes it clear that what Angelhoff calls "revolutionary action" (282) is actually an instance of the self-defeat of socialism: the promising student flees to West Germany feeling — not without reason — threatened by the far-reaching suspicions of his teacher. That the references to panegyric praises of Stalin are thoroughly ironic is supported by the sarcastic references to Stalin found elsewhere.

More generally speaking, Kant criticizes simplistic "Agitprop" lyrics, i. e. lyrics written for the sake of "agitation and propaganda." In a hilarious scene, Iswall and his friends compose an "October March" (108 ff.). In this scene, Kant's parodistic technique can be demonstrated in detail. The young students composing this text collectively are only too prone to pour their genuine enthusiasm into stereotyped molds. They discover for themselves that the suggested line "we die for the Republic" is hollow in its defiance of death; and Kant, therefore, has them agree on the "less sectarian" lines "Sterben will keiner, aber leben will jeder, darum nun Schluß mit dem Krieg!" ("No one wants to die, everyone wants to live; therefore away now with war!" 109).

Another idea for the song being composed is "greift in die Räder" ("grab hold of the wheels"). The metonymic use of *Rad* or *Räder* for the economy, especially the representation of the mechanized, industrial production through "turning wheels" is well established. One might be reminded of Georg Herwegh's early expression of proletarian self-confidence in his "Bundeslied":

> Alle Räder stehen still,
> Wenn dein starker Arm es will.
>
> All the wheels will soon stand still,
> If your strong arms do so will.

The suggested line "Greift nun zum Hammer und greift in die Räder" contains this stereotyped metaphor in an ambiguous construction; this line would either call for devotion to work or for sabotage (109 f.). The ambiguity is discovered when one of the students points out:

> "...Da kann man reingreifen, um sie zu drehen oder um sie anzuhalten; das führt zu Mißverständnissen."
>
> "...You can grab hold of them and either turn them or stop them; that leads to misunderstandings."

Here Kant exposes in an amusing way the hollowness of a kind of literature in which pre-formulated clichés are pieced together. Other stereotypes do find their way into the final draft of the "October March," including the metaphoric use of hammer and pen for manual and intellectual work, respectively; the rejection of "Krieg" (war), coupled with (and even rhyming with) the certainty of "Sieg" (victory); and the rhythmic change, in the last line, from the former iambic and dactylic rhythms into trochaeic rhythm. It should not be overlooked, however, that Kant combines here as elsewhere criticism of form with assertion of content elements.

The *Aula* contains a long episode satirizing the literary establishment of East Germany by describing a meeting of East Germany's "Writers' Union" (Deutscher Schriftstellerverband). Here Kant displays a fireworks of wit to highlight certain questionable aspects of East Germany's literary scene. Among the objects of his satire are bureaucratic elements in literary life, the "generation gap" between authors, the annoying support of untalented "young talents," low quality literary criticism, and Party interference with the production of plays (335 ff.). In this episode also, Kant humorously questions the so-called "Bitterfelder Weg" (Bitterfeld Movement) as to its goals and achievements. There are numerous examples here of direct and indirect literary references. To name just one: Kant uses several "significant names," e. g. *Bertold Wassermann* and *Buchhacker.* The second name may be translated as "book-hatcheter" or "book-axer." Furthermore, an incompetent critic is called *Schlichtkow,* which is equivalent to something like "McPlain." These "significant names" may themselves be tongue-in-cheek references to Strittmatter (and other socialist writers) who uses this technique abundantly in his popular novel *Ole Bienkopp.*

Throughout the world Bertolt Brecht is probably the best-known figure of East Germany's early literary scene. On the other hand, he continues to be controversial in the socialist countries, or at least a continuing source of irritation to the Party-line cultural bureaucrats. Brecht had been struggling with — and against — the principles of Socialist Realism from the very beginning of his turning to the cause of marxism. While working at his Berlin "Theater am Schiffbauerdamm," he had several arguments with the official authorities in literature and theater; the greatest publicity was probably received by the 1952 events surrounding his play *Lucullus* which was attacked as being too "formalistic." This attack was based on the "Declaration Against Decadence and Formalism" which the Party had issued in 1951, and on the basis of which the works of Kafka and Benn had been virtually banned.[4]

Brecht agreed after long discussions with Party officials to alter the message of his drama "Das Verhör des Lukullus" (*The Interrogation of Lucullus*), the last original play completed by Brecht. The new version had the title "Die Verurteilung des Lukullus" (*The Sentencing of Lucullus*), but still did not satisfy the cultural authorities.

The above events are alluded to in the *Aula* by a stalinist teacher telling his students that they should "please to use the power of their lungs in the fight against decadence, *Lucullus* for example, or something like that" ("mochten sie ihre Puste gefälligst im Kampf gegen die Dekadenz einsetzen, 'Lukullus' oder so etwas," 394).

Even more specifically, Kant may allude to the futile attempt of the East Berlin authorities to have the first performance of Brecht's revised "Lucullus" booed off the stage by distributing tickets to that performance to reliable members of communist youth organizations; however, the performance turned out to be a startling success, partly because many of the young people sold their free tickets to Brecht "fans" and West Berlin critics.

References to Brecht underscore the importance of this author to Iswall. To give an example: when studying literature in Berlin, Iswall saw Brecht's "The Caucasian Chalk Circle" six times and "Mother Courage" even more frequently (402).

Brecht's peom "Fragen eines lesenden Arbeiters" is used as a leitmotif representing in a nutshell the principles of the new educational orientation in East Germany. The poem is introduced to the workers'-and-peasants' students by the idealized teacher Riebenlamm as a "first rule" for their outlook on history (80 ff.; compare further 436). Riebenlamm uses this poem in a hearty way as a basic piece of enlightenment: "Now you are beginning to see the light." ("Euch hat einer ein Licht aufgesteckt," 81).

It seems significant that Kant chose this poem as a literary leitmotif. It consists almost entirely of questions asking who actually performed the great deeds in history — the famous great men or the masses upon whom they were depending in every respect. In connection with this poem, the teacher emphasizes the importance of questioning and doubting; highest praise is given to a student who dares to ask a critical question beginning with *but*, although the objection itself does not hold (81). The scene reminds one of another Brecht poem which says "Those who inquire about something, deserve an answer" — "Die etwas fragen, / Die verdienen Antwort" (from "Legende von der Entstehung des Buches Taoteking"). The poem "Fragen eines lesenden Arbeiters" is taken up by Riebenlamm during the discussion of the problematical China scholarship; he refers to the question of where the masons went on the evening that the Great Chinese Wall was completed, and suggests jokingly that "at least one of the questions of the reading worker could be answered on the spot," if Gerd and his classmate Rose were to accept this scholarship (436). In this connection, the word *Mauerbau* is used, too. It is tempting to speculate what Kant is implying, since probably no East German author writing after the building of the Berlin Wall (August 13, 1961) can use the word "Mauerbau" (or even "Der Bau," which is the title of a drama by Heiner Müller)[65] without knowing that a connection will be drawn to this event. However, there is no clear evidence as to these implications; even where the Berlin Wall is directly mentioned, it is done in a matter-of-fact way, reflecting upon Germany's borders at the time of Heine's "Deutschland, ein Wintermärchen," upon the borders in the Germany immediately after the war, and upon the differences between what is going on east and west of this border (54 f.). The Wall itself is neither defended nor attacked — which may be a message in itself.

There are further allusions to Brecht's works. On his way to clearing up a dark point in his past, Iswall drives over a former glacial mountain range, and seeing the idyllic countryside, he criticizes convocation speakers who are "sweet, cultivated, and without memories of glaciers and icy times" ("lieblich, kultiviert und ohne Erinnerungen an Gletscher und eisige Zeiten," 409). "Eisige Zeiten" brings to mind several poems by Brecht, mainly the early "Vom armen B. B." and the late "An die Nachgeborenen." The symbolism of coming over mountains or forgetting that one did come over the mountains (the word *Gebirge* occurs four times, 409; compare also "eiszeitliches Hochgebirge" further down, 460) alludes to Brecht's masterly, succinct formulation of what is a basic thought in Kant's *Aula*:

Die Mühen der Gebirge liegen hinter uns,
Vor uns liegen die Mühen der Ebenen. [66]

The troubles of the mountains are behind us,
Before us are the troubles of the plains.

In his study on East German poetry, John Flores emphasizes the influence Brecht exerted with his "critical stance" upon East German literature, particularly on poetry.[67] It is interesting that Brecht, as shown in the case of the *Aula*, also exerted important influence upon prose literature. Brecht's influence is probably based in part on the fact that his critical stance included an element of openness, insistence upon continuing change, and thus undogmatic self-criticism. It must be remembered that criticism and self-criticism form part of the communist dogma, and that, on the other hand, the "permanent revolution" is a formula denouncing the Social Democrats and other "revisionists." Thus, while claiming the authority of the socialist "classic" Brecht, an author may espouse ideas that could, without such a reference, easily be called revisionistic.

Non-socialist literature

After having discussed examples and aspects of Kant's critical look at the East German literary scene, I would like to turn to his references to non-socialist literature. In the area of what is generally called "trivial literature," the *Aula* offers several interesting observations.

Kant has his hero Iswall read a pocket book by Raymond Chandler while returning from Hamburg by train. Here Kant offers an amusing parody of Chandler as a representative of Western mass culture. In this scene he has Iswall observe a situation through the eyes of Chandler, the strong language of his inner comments being a far cry from his usual style. Iswall uses several curse words; in an imagined answer of Chandler's, we find three times the word *gottverdammt* (goddamn), e. g. in the combination "dieses gottverdammte Stinktier von einer Katze" ("this goddamned skunk of a cat," 227) with regard to a fellow passenger's cat. Thus, while rejecting Chandler and what he stands for in the end, Kant still allows him to contribute one more facet to the varieties of style in the *Aula*.

At another place, Kant compares Iswall's facing of his own past with a showdown in American movies and uses this opportunity to give a brilliant description of the typical showdown of a Western (407 f.).

Kant suggests that popular fiction, even non-socialist products, may have more merits than a socialist purist would admit. This interpretation is supported by several allusions to Karl May where Iswall stands up for the admired author of his youth (cf. 420 f.; see also 88, where Winnetou and Shatterhand are mentioned). In his typically exaggerated manner, Iswall sings rhapsodic praises of Karl May: "O herrlicher sächsischer Lügenbold, gepriesen sei dein vielgeschmähter Name!" Iswall sees any ideological shortcomings of May outweighed by far by the value this author had for him. As for specific "disparagings of May's name," Iswall mentions the allegations that May is "religious-sentimental" and "nationalistic" — objections which Iswall modifies, questions, and even ridicules. Later on in this episode, Iswall scorns hypocrisy about May's work: a man who looks like a higher cultural functionary speaks disdainfully of May, does not admit to reading May, and the same man, Iswall muses, will chide his wife for not coming to grips with Sholokhov's *The Quiet Don* (422). The following antithesis capsules neatly Iswall's opinion of May, his attitude to the official verdict on May, and his opinion of hypocritical readers of May: "He is a likeable man who reads Karl May, and an unlikeable guy who denies it." ("Es war ein sympathischer Mensch, der Karl May liest, und ein unsympathischer Kerl, der's leugnet," 422).

Although disdainfully discarded as "trivial literature" by academic authorities in East and West Germany, the works of Karl May still exert a tremendous influence on German culture. According to an article in the German weekly *Der Spiegel*, Karl May's works have made deeper imprints on Germany than did any other writer between Goethe and Thomas Mann.[68]

Kant refuses to simplify historic developments in retrospect, and even ridicules inept attempts at expurgating any literature that does not measure up to the yardstick used by cultural authorities. He comes close to an idea expressed by Leslie Fiedler with reference to "bad poems":

> Bad poems tell a special kind of truth about the past which we cannot do without. A nation which expurgates from its anthologies those great bad poems it has loved, quite like a nation which refuses to include in those anthologies its great ones, is a nation with only half a memory.[69]

Classical literature

I have shown how Kant implicitly criticizes and modifies the officially established judgment on contemporary socialist and non-socialist literature. Equally differentiated are his references to the "classics," to the accepted works of world literature. No attempt is made here at an exhaustive enumeration of all references and allusions; rather, typical examples representing a particular function of such references will be singled out and discussed. As a rule, the allusion is interwoven into the plot; since the "monkey Iswall" is choosing and adapting the respective motif, the form is entertaining parody; the reference is comically inadequate, and yet there is some appeal to the classical authority — even if this classical authority challenges some officially maintained opinion.

As mentioned earlier, the theory of Socialist Realism presently accepted in East Germany has it that their socialist society is the true guardian and follower of all previous "progressive" literature, in particular of the German "patriotic" classics. This claim leads easily to a mechanical, bureaucratic approach to cultural heritage. Kant mocks this approach in an episode in which some of the proletarian students are "delegated to receive cultural heritage," as the official records have it. ("Sie seien ... die Delegation einer Arbeiter-und-Bauern-Fakultät, abgeordnet zur Entgegennahme von Kulturerbe," 370.) The very wording ridicules the inadequacy of this attitude towards culture. In the course of this episode, Kant makes it clear that "the phenomenon J. S. Bach" cannot be captured with a few marxist terms, and that "reception of cultural heritage" is a rather complex process. The man who suggests to capsule Bach as "Bauernkrieg, Bürgertum und Mathematik" ("the Peasant Insurrection, bourgeoisie, and mathematics," 372) is Völschow, the stalinist whose dogmatism is combined with Prussian idealism and sense of duty.

Several important literary references are connected with the study of literature during Iswall's condensed high-school curriculum at his "Workers' and Peasants' College," e. g. Gottfried Keller's "Abendlied" (111). In a hilarious scene, the somewhat old-fashioned, but not entirely negative German teacher tries hard to make his proletarian students acquainted with Keller, as he sees him. We see the class grope for words to communicate their impressions; Kant adds a comical flair of class war to the scene in that the "bourgeois" teacher refuses to take Keller's atheism seriously. The teacher is more and more cornered by the perceptive, if a bit inarticulate, class, and finally resorts to an appeal to their aesthetic sense, asking them if they don't at least admit that the last two lines are beautiful:

> Trinkt, o Augen, was die Wimper hält,
> Von dem goldnen Überfluß der Welt! (114)

> Drink, o eyes, whate'er your lash will hold,
> Of the wells of this world's liquid gold! (114)

The class agrees, and the episode closes on this conciliatory note.

In the above scene, it becomes clear that Kant endorses whole-heartedly the goal to open the treasures of classical literature to the people. He openly admits difficulties in this process of emancipation and acculturation, but shows also that a fresh, spontaneous approach to this literature has the chance to avoid or correct common misjudgments.

The motif of Keller's "Evening Song" is later continued in a pun on a suspected exchange of glances: "Trullesand's and Vera Bilfert's eyes, whose glances caused you [Iswall, T. L.] to play God and Fate and historical necessity." ("Trullesands und Vera Bilferts Augen, auf deren Schein hin du den lieben Gott gespielt hast und Schicksal und historische Notwendigkeit," 422.) "To play historical necessity" is a play on one of the basic marxistic tenets; in the situation, it is motivated and softened by the pun on Keller's poem and by the parallels to the idioms "lieber Gott spielen" und "Schicksal spielen."

It is tempting to look for further-reaching parallels between Keller and Kant, especially since Kant has Iswall call Keller and himself "Germany's greatest poets" (168). Although comically out of place, this statement may hint at Kant owing Keller more than just a few motifs.

A reference to Goethe's "Prometheus" provides an example of Kant's "critical stance" towards naive or cynical socialist optimism.[70] In the context of socialism, Goethe's famous poem can be interpreted as a poetic version of the socialist attempt to "form a new man" after the image of true man as described in the writings of the marxistic classics. In the *Aula*, however, this poem is connected with negative sides of the formation of a new society: the man who praises Goethe as someone from whom "you can learn a lot" (357), the Spanish Civil War veteran Haiduck, is himself an example of "blossoming dreams that did not bear fruit"; his hope for a "particular way of Germany to socialism" was not fulfilled, and his career was interrupted when he refused to deny ever having had such views. Furthermore, the recital of this poem follows a talk about the apparent defection of a highly talented student to the West.

Kant uses the authority of classical literature to comment on conflicts both of the socialist society as a whole and of the individual in such a society. Socialist doctrine has it that in a socialist society any conflicts can only be of a "non-antagonistical" and thereby of a radically different nature than in any other society. This optimistic and rationalistic approach, in its simplified form, regards the irrational in man only as a "relic

94

of bourgeois thinking." In one of the central episodes of the *Aula*, the irrational plays a major part: Iswall betrays his best friend out of jealousy. When reflecting upon that situation, he sees himself transformed into King Marke of Cornwallis, the Moor of Venice, and Richard III (432). The comparison with Marke is continued through the term *Tristaniaden* (437); and, at another place, the betrayal of his friend is paralleled to Hagen's murder of Siegfried (305).

The Faust motif, too, is connected with this central conflict between friendship and love, between communist solidarity and irrational egoism. In Iswall's reflections, we find a passage that seems at first glance to be just a playful allusion to Goethe's *Faust* and to Thomas Mann's *Doktor Faustus*:

> der Leipziger Doktor ist nur knapp davongekommen, der Musikant aus Kaisersaschern aber keineswegs, der ist zur Hölle gefahren und dazu hat's getönt, als wär's von Arnold Schönberg — (433)

> The Leipzig doctor barely escaped, but the musician from Kaisersaschern not at all; he went to hell, accompanied by sounds that could have been from Arnold Schönberg — (433)

Here, Kant plays with two great versions of the Faust motif; and, in the case of Adrian Leverkühn, allows himself an allusion to Schönberg, who was, as will be remembered, the model of music history for Mann's *Faustus*, an allusion which appears to be a stricture against modern music.

What is implied here is a comparison of Iswall to Faust. While trying to explain to himself his act of jealousy, Iswall feels compelled to assume a scheming by the devil. By pointing out great men who fell victim to the devil, Iswall excuses his own failure; the extended devil metaphor calls upon the reader to find the real reasons behind Iswall's behavior, since obviously a marxist has to go beyond such mythological verbiage.

As far as the Faust motif itself is concerned, one may also find here an allusion to the long drawn-out public discussion of the "real historical meaning" of the Faust character, which was triggered by a fragmentary Faust libretto by Hanns Eisler. Eisler's script describes Faust's turning to philosophy as an escape from his responsibilities towards the cause of the rebellious peasants.[71] Faust's reversal would exactly parallel Luther's denouncement of the revolutionary peasants, which is referred to several times in the *Aula*, as in the phrase "die verräterische Nachtigall" (the treacherous nightingale of Wittenberg, 70). Luther is also the third great man listed in the above-mentioned episode where "things turned out badly" through the devil's interference.

As a last, but by no means least influence, the author Heinrich Heine must be mentioned. The *Aula* is prefaced by a motto from Heine:

> Der heutige Tag ist
> ein Resultat des gestrigen.
> Was dieser gewollt hat,
> müssen wir erforschen,
> wenn wir zu wissen wünschen,
> was jener will.

> This day is
> a result of yesterday.
> What the latter demanded,
> we must investigate,
> if we wish to know
> what this day demands.

In the context of the novel, this motto appears to be directed against a naive "orientation towards the future," as espoused mainly by Direktor Meibaum. In his letter to the first graduating class of the Workers' and Peasants' College, this Party official denounces as negative what the Heine motto regards as necessary for knowledge of today's challenges: Meibaum claims that the character of the tentative program had been too "retrospective" (*rückwärtsgewandt*), contrasts this with a program which "gets its bearings from the new and from the tasks lying ahead," and announces that instead of the commemorative convocation in the Aula, there will be lectures on socialist university politics (458). The "orientation towards the new" is repeated and varied several times polemically (459, 462). Furthermore, this motto is taken up several times as at theme. When Iswall receives the request for the Aula speech, he speaks, in the course of lengthy reflections, of the "trivial truth" that one cannot have a future without a past: the real problem is *how* to speak of the past (10 f.).

Stalin is quoted as having said that one must forget the past, if one is to gain the future.[72] The theologian referring to Stalin drew the parallel to the biblical image of the tiller who was not to look back; other parallels could be added. Whether or not Kant alluded to a specific saying by Stalin or some other communist leader, his whole book is a refusal to forget the past and sacrifice the present for the future.

The *Aula*'s motto quoted above is markedly unrevolutionary, or revolutionary in a sober, non-fanatical, even self-critical sense; so are the other references to Heine. In his conversation with the Hamburg merchant Windshull, Iswall and his partner try to counter each other's ideological arguments with Heine quotes. Both claim that their society is heeding the advice Heine gave in his "Wintermärchen" to the city of Hamburg after the catastrophic fire of 1842:

> Baut eure Häuser wieder auf
> und trocknet eure Pfützen
> und schafft euch bessre Gesetze an
> und bessre Feuerspritzen. (138 f.)

> Rebuild, what has been burnt with fire
> and dry the puddles left;
> and better laws you should acquire,
> and better fire-fighting jets. (138 f.)

In this witty conversation, neither of the two discussants abandons his position, and neither wins out openly, although it is suggested that Iswall's arguments are, in the final analysis, stronger. The situation, too, if taken as typical for the West German system, would support Iswall's standpoint: the scene takes place immediately after the flood catastrophe in Hamburg in Spring 1962. Windshull has the last word in the conversation, "And you are a dogmatic," to which Iswall replies: "Cheers!"; "and also Herr Windshull said: 'Cheers!'" (141). The ideological gulf is bridged momentarily by the common ground of their allegiance to Heine; in such an atmosphere of humor, the basic disagreements are not forgotten, but temporarily suspended.

In one of his reflections on sending Trullesand to China, Iswall reduces the problem to the "abstract figure" that "someone did not get the girl, because someone else also had wanted her and did get her," (312 f.). Here, one finds another reference to Heine; one feels strongly reminded of Heine's repeated motto in his *Ideen. Das Buch Le Grand.*

Iswall extends the allusion to Heine, calling the event an "ancient drama in the theater of mankind" ("Ur-Stück im Menschentheater"). Hermand speaks, with reference to this passage, of the existence of a human "Urseele"; and indeed, Kant seems to acknowledge here certain unchanging irrational constancies in the human psyche.[73]

Heine's influence on Kant extends beyond direct references. Like Heine, Kant will confront romantic illusions with the harshness of reality; however, Kant's anti-romantic turns are much less cutting than Heine's (cf. 125 ff., 413 ff.).

Thus, literary references play an important role in the style, structure, and theme of the *Aula*; these references document and characterize, parody polemically, contribute humorous and comical elements, and fulfill structural functions as leitmotifs. Since Kant-Iswall is rather sceptical about authorities, his quotations very rarely invoke a literary source in a simple way as a witness for universal truth, or as a giver of an unquestioned answer. One of these rare cases is the leitmotivic reference to Brecht's poem **"Fragen eines lesenden Arbeiters,"** but the "truth" of this poem — and of other references to Brecht's works — has been shown to be that it is necessary to go on asking questions, to continue the never-ending task of emancipation. And if Kant characterizes the barbarism of the Nazis by the term *Bücherverbrenner* (55), we may assume that Kant envisages a higher stage of emancipation in his society at which time authors like Kafka will be fully accessible to the people to be read or to be rejected. Several allusions to Kafka both in the *Aula* and in Kant's most recent novel *Das Impressum* suggest this conclusion; it is not that Kant stands up for the denounced Kafka, but he does question and ridicule his suppression. This interpretation is supported by an episode from Kant's *Impressum*, which is dialectical humor crystallized: namely, a man who is characterized as being rather narrow-minded becomes proverbial with his verdict on Kafka:

Die Verwandlung eines Menschen in einen Käfer
ist für uns keine annehmbare Lösung![74]

The metamorphosis of a human being into a
beetle is for us no acceptable solution!

KANT'S *AULA* — HUMOROUS REFLECTIONS ON THE DIALECTICS OF OLD AND NEW

In this last chapter I would like to present further observations and summarize the main ideas of this study. The following summaries and generalizations are necessarily less conclusive than the preceding formal analyses. However, since even the relatively objective analyses will be influenced by the writer's subjectivity, it can be helpful if some of these subjective opinions are stated openly.

Dialectical humor as the aesthetic conscience of Socialist Realism

To which extent, or in which sense, can the *Aula* be classified as a work of Socialist Realism? In East Germany, it is taken for granted that Kant's works are in the tradition of Socialist Realism, whereas Western observers tend to pay little, if any, attention to this theory. Thus, it seems in place to clarify the above question.

Much in Kant's novel, it seems, has to be understood as polemics against too narrow an understanding of the theory of Socialist Realism. As mentioned before, Kant satirizes rather openly the kind of shallow, poorly written literature that is accepted and promoted in East Germany.

Iswall "bekommt Schluckbeschwerden" ("gets the hiccups") when he rereads after a lapse of ten years or so his last college essay; for in it he comes to the conclusion that the Soviet author Tchakovsky, in his novel "Bei uns ist schon Morgen" (*Where We Are, Morning Has Already Dawned*), "fulfills the five requirements of Socialist Realism in every respect," (244 f.). In another essay, he reads that Socialist Realism was "invented by Gorki," a statement which was modified by the teacher in the margin to read that Gorki had "elaborated Socialist Realism in practical-poetical fashion," (245).

Obviously here, Kant is ridiculing a narrow, mechanistic interpretation of art; in particular, since the essays are dated 1951, Kant is criticizing the enforcement of blind aesthetic principles in the Stalin era.

The mechanical application of certain rules and principles is also criticized elsewhere (cf. 14, 33 f., 108 f., 266, 285 ff., 349). Underdeveloped or degenerated forms of Socialist Realism are also criticized in the lengthy episode dealing with the Writers' Union meeting (335 ff.). Among other things, Kant mocks, in a hilarious mystification, an aesthetic theory which centers around a "cat"; this "cat" has about the same function as the "falcon" in Heyse's theory of the novella, the problem being that this "cat" eludes all efforts of concretization and verification.

The Schlenstedts see in the motif of the "Waterman Cat" a criticism of a simplified theory of narration, and, more generally, claim that Kant criticizes here the phenomenon that certain methods which are useful for specific artistic purposes become dogma and thus useless abstractions ("jegliche Dogmatisierung einmal gewonnener, für bestimmte Gestaltungen geeigneter Methoden zu nutzlosen Abstrakta").[75]

I agree with the Schlenstedts in the above case, but would like to leave the question open as to the range of literary concepts and products on which this verdict is passed. Among other things, the "Principle of the Waterman Cat" is probably a parody of Becher's "prägnanter Punkt," a vaguely defined central idea of Becher's aesthetic theory which refers to the inner totality or specific harmony that characterizes the real work of art.

Kant ist not the first to point out misconceptions and distortions of Socialist Realism, and to plead for self-criticism and differentiation. Also in various "guidelines" and "orientation helps" issued by the Party, the point is stressed that artists should themselves be their sharpest critics, and that they should overcome everything unfinished, dishonest, or unclear; that, in close connection with the working class and its Party, they should strive to see the real nature of things; that they should not avoid tough problems; and that they should not offer cheap solutions to conflicts. Too, there is often reference to the "role" or function of literature, namely to appeal to both the intellect and the emotions of the reader and thus to challenge him to find adequate socialistic responses. And by now in the socialist countries, Socialist Realism is considered to be an emerging and developing tradition rather than a readily applicable set of rules; the importance of the respective artistic medium within the "ensemble" of all the other arts is stressed, and the contribution of the artist's unique individuality is more acknowledged than before.

Fitting Kant into this interpretation of Socialist Realism, his aesthetic position could well be stated as follows: literature should be typical, but not stereotyped; the author has reason to be optimistic, but he should remain critically aware of conflicts and unsolved problems; the point of view should be the emerging socialist order, but without dogmatic fanaticism; the style should be popular, but avoid clichés and oversimplifications; and the author should always be aware of the moral and educational functions of literature.

Yet, although no part of the above description seems unfitting, the formula as a whole severely distorts the aesthetic position inherent in the *Aula*; such a formula would regard dialectical humor only as an embellishment of the formal side, assigning it a function in a mechanical, normative theory. Dialectical humor, however, as this concept has been developed here, transcends any normative theory; indeed, it challenges the priority of aesthetic theory over literary practice. As a marxist, Kant is, of course, far from claiming art to exist for art's sake; as Brecht put it once, art cannot possess autarchy, but its autonomy should be recognized.

The function of structural openness

In the light of the preceding argument, multifunctionality and structural openness assume a deeper, dynamic meaning: the theory and practice of Socialist Realism has always been in danger of regarding the truth of literature as a rather direct function of the truth of the marxist-leninist doctrines, whereas Kant emphasizes through the very form of his art that truth is not so easily disposable. For the sake of the full truth, every action has to be seen together with its causes and consequences for all persons involved:

> Die Wahrheit aber ist nicht nur die Tat, sondern auch deren Folge, nicht nur Motiv, sondern auch Wirkung, ist Vorsatz und Ergebnis; die Wahrheit sind auch die anderen. (409)

Iswall objects to putting "paint on the cracks" (409), and he speaks of a "missing dimension" in movies, where the actual, concrete situations of individuals are neglected (293 ff.). It is only consequential that curiosity is given great importance (187, 408); and Riebenlamm, the idealized teacher, praises profusely a student who dares to voice a thought beginning with *aber* (81), although the student's objection does not hold. Kant does not boast the possession of truth, but rather shows his characters in the process of searching for truth; he does not celebrate the arrival at a promised state, but rather points out stations on the contradictory way in what appears to be the right direction.

The above passages are interesting as support for the view expressed here, but more important is the analysis of the forms in which Kant's basic dialectical thinking is embodied. Such analyses have already been provided in this study for various areas of the *Aula*'s style and structure; at this point, it seems in place to take up once again the questions of the *Aula*'s narrative structure.

The paper by the Schlenstedts, which contributes valuable detailed insights into the *Aula*'s narrative structure, refers to Kant's basic point of view as "epic irony," a concept which bears certain similarities to what is here called dialectical humor.[76] However, for the Schlenstedts the core of "epic irony" consists in the "elevated standpoint" which Kant is gaining for himself and for the reader; and their criticism is that this irony is not "fully achieved":

> Frequently, the author does not succeed in evaluating unclarified matters from a higher stage of the development, nor in characterizing Iswall's inconsistencies as such, but he merely reproduces them.[77]

> Oft erreicht es der Autor nämlich nicht, das unklar Bleibende von höherer Stufe aus zu werten, die Inkonsequenzen Iswalls als solche zu charakterisieren, sondern er reproduziert sie einfach.

It appears, however, that within the framework of present-day socialist aesthetics, the insistence upon the author's elevated standpoint or higher point of view has an apologetic and even a progressive function: towards the end of their paper, the Schlenstedts acknowledge Kant's polemics against several kinds of aesthetic "freezes" (*Erstarrungen*) and call Kant's use of modern literary forms and techniques an immanent polemics in the same direction. These modern formal elements were, in the early post-war phase, banned as decadent; however, if "used by a socialist for the construction of a systematic and structure-giving world-view, these forms change their function and thereby their character."[78]

As for shortcomings of Kant's "epic irony," the Schlenstedts criticize "lack of intensive totality" in several characters, as well as his technique of artistic spontaneity; more specifically, Kant's critics object to ideological discussions being left unfinished,[79] and complain that the satiric description of the Writers' Union meeting "illuminates the panorama only partially."[80] It would seem that the Schlenstedts, who otherwise go along with Kant's criticism of dogmatic distortions in East Germany's immediate past, fall back at this point themselves into a dogmatic position: on the basis of aesthetic norms, certain literary techniques and structures are justified, others rejected.

Antithetical composition

It is in keeping with the approach followed in this study to say that also structure and composition are characterized by significant openness; seemingly isolated anecdotes, abrupt transitions, missing links, and unmotivated flashbacks turn out to be instances of dialectical humor in the area of structure.

It was mentioned in chapter two that Iswall's "monkeyness" has structural consequences; frequently, Iswall allows himself to indulge in exaggerated praise or criticism which he himself or someone else then immediately corrects. This dialectical thought development is not restricted to large thought units, but can be observed an lower levels, for example in the formation of phrases and sentences. In structuring a textual unit, Kant shows a preference for contrasts and negations. On pages 76 and 77 alone, Kant uses sixteen times the negation *nicht*, five other negatives, and ten restrictive conjunctions (*aber, doch, sondern*). Some further contrasts are not expressed overtly. It seems significant that the pattern *nicht / aber* is more frequent than *nicht / sondern. Nicht / aber* leaves thesis and antithesis unreconciled, whereas the peremptory *sondern* tends to cancel the original thesis.

Many of the antithetical contrasts assume a humorous character because of some inherent inadequacy, as when Iswall associates the two slogans "Kraftfahrer, haltet Abstand!" and "Journalisten, näher ans Leben!" (33). Both the traffic rule to keep distance and the advice to reporters to get closer to life have a well-defined meaning in their respective spheres; juxtaposing them on the basis of their common feature of proximity creates

a comical effect, since traffic and journalism are unrelated areas of life.
It is left to the reader to evaluate both slogans, especially the second
one. In context, this antithesis is used as a transition to a serious thought;
for Iswall it is a means to question himself as to how "close to life"
he, a journalist, really is, causing him to neglect his present duties and
immerse himself in reflections upon the past.

Occasionally, the author Kant uses associative concatenation of scenes
in a playful way. Thus, a real policeman interrupts Iswall's memories
of an episode in which the career of a policeman is mentioned as a
"genuine alternative" for Iswall — an alternative which he does not choose
(31 f.).

It is characteristic of Kant's dialectical thinking that he emphasizes
the contradiction between thesis and antithesis rather than the harmony
of a synthesis. A synthesis is at best implied; or if a synthesis is reached,
it usually provokes a new antithesis. One function of these continuous
contrasts and contradictions is to point out the complexities of reality:
with every negation, Kant shows an objective possibility which could
have been chosen instead of the other possibility which actually became
reality.

Different time levels are also used as a device of dialectical humor.
As Hermand noted, Kant leaves it frequently open as to whether he
is really speaking of the early post-war time or of his own present time
of the sixties.[81] This observation can be expanded: not only are the
relationships between the time levels not made explicit, but both time
levels are shown to be complex themselves, possessing their specific
positive and negative features. The early time seems to have more
enthusiasm, despite the crude methods used in certain instances by the
persons and institutions who had gained power; as for the episodes from
Kant's present time, there is evidence of positive consequences of the
de-stalinization, but also, Kant suggests, there are new problems, such
as the increasing pressure put on people to "qualify" themselves for
promotion in their jobs, and an annoying expansion — or re-establishment
— of bureaucracy (see especially page 405 ff.).

Complexity and multivalence are also characteristic of most leitmotifs.
The dialectics of the old and the new finds an adequate representation
in the leitmotivic symbol of the university auditorium, the "Aula." This
tradition-burdened convocation hall had been built as a library centuries
ago. For a bourgeois student parlamentarian, this witness of feudal times

is the symbol of the conservative virtues of the city; for the students of the new "Workers' and Peasants' College," the "Aula" is the place of their struggles, witnessing success and failure. It seems obvious that the "Aula" then is a well-chosen symbol for the new students' take-over of the heritage of the past, but it is worth-while to have a closer look at the implied dialectics of the old and the new.

The Aula motif is introduced early in the novel. After the brief exposition in which Iswall receives the invitation for his Aula speech, his thoughts go back to his and his friend's first encounter with this building. Even the word *Aula* is unknown to the carpenter Trullesand (9). This first confrontation with their future university shows already that gaining access to former privileges is a complex process: it is subjectively frightening and objectively difficult; the new students meet indeed with condescendence or even rejection of the traditional establishment, yet they are praiseworthy representatives of a new order granting long over-due chances of equality. At the same time, this emancipatory process could endanger its very goals, as the revolutionary imagery of "taking it by storm-attack" suggests.

In the description of the "Aula," there is criticism of medieval social conditions involved, as when Kant speaks of the "costly pride of the dukes of Pommerania-Wolgast" (9). All further references to "Andreas Meyer's Aula" and to details of its architecture and precious art-works resound this critical note; thus, whether it is intended or not, the motif of the Aula implies that cultural heritage includes inheritance of guilt.

From yet another point of view, the "Aula" is a concrete symbol of the lingering superiority of the former social order. In the student election campaign held in the Aula, the conservative student praises this building as the "calm eye in all of history's whirl-winds" (212); and it is only through traditional rhetorical means that one of the proletarian students is admitted as a candidate (216 ff.). Riek's pose of Athenian eloquence has clearly comical functions; yet he himself wonders why this kind of detour is more successful than the concise propaganda slogans he and his comrades had offered at first to the audience (219).

The *Aula* closes with Iswall's musings about the cancelling of his Aula speech. The fact that he is not allowed to deliver his speech is clearly a flaw in the development of the socialist society that Kant has been tracing in this highly subjective book; on the other hand, Iswall says that he is not "wrathful," and the whole scene suggests that actually, the novel itself is Iswall's speech, delivered to a far greater audience than a real speech at his university could have reached. In summary, one can say that the leitmotif "Aula" is witness and symbol of positive and negative sides of both the old and the new.

Limitations of dialectical humor

Dialectical humor does impose, on the other hand, certain limitations and restrictions upon the artist. The choice of Robert Iswall as "quasi-narrator" entails pervasive humorous subjectivity and intellectuality; the *Aula* is intellectual to such an extent that the atmospheric and lyrical details are omitted, unless they can be exploited for some humorous contrast. Thus, there is some justification for the judgment that several of Kant's characters lack "intensive totality." [82] Indeed, Kant does not achieve "intensive Totalität" in any of his characters — but then, he does not claim to, either. It would be equally wrong to say that Kant uses his characters only as vehicles for the expression of ideas, or as allegorical figures in the dramatization of certain conflicts; his characters — at least most of the more important ones — do possess individuality, but not more than is compatible with the basic pattern of dialectical humor.

Kant is aware of the fact that his novel concentrates on comical contrasts, excluding the sum of circumstances which would relativize — or even neutralize — the instantaneous humor. The deeper and darker aspects of life are underplayed: passions, sufferings, sickness and death are not excluded, yet rarely if ever are they given full attention either. These restrictions are the price of a humorous position; at times, Kant-Iswall even experiences the deeper plight of all humorists — the plight of not being taken seriously.

In a discussion about what is funny about jokes, Kant has the protagonists of his novel express various opinions which, taken together and interpreted with caution, seem to reflect the author's aesthetic position. The discussion circles around the question as to when a story ceases to be funny, especially when the circumstances are as sad as in the case of World War II, for example (376). One conclusion is:

> Man kann ja was wissen, muß aber nicht immer dran denken, ... das kann ja gar keiner: immer an alles denken. Immer an alles denken, macht einen verrückt. Dann gibt's überhaupt nichts Lustiges mehr. (376 f.)

> You can know something, but you don't have to think of it all
> the time, ... that is not possible: to think of everything all the time.
> To think of everything all the time drives you crazy. Then there's
> nothing at all funny any more. (376 f.)

This statement is further modified: in some instances it is not possible
to forget the circumstances. This is the case with the bourgeois
"Oberförster" who tried to be "funny" at a party with a paper-maché
nose; but with him, it was not possible to forget that he was a "pig"
(377).

Kant recognizes the existence of limitations on humor; however, after
what has been said thus far about Kant's aesthetics, these limits cannot
be expected to be drawn very clearly. Kant somehow deliberately blurs
the distinction between real life and its artistic representation. In the
discussion just referred to, Kant uses the ambiguous word *Geschichte*
("story"): the "real" Oberförster is not funny, but the story about him
is. Iswall himself says early in that discussion: "A good story is good,
no matter what" ("Wenn eine Geschichte gut ist, geht sie nicht kaputt,"
375).

Seen in context, this cannot mean that aesthetic principles are completely
self-sufficient, that Kant advocates the opinion that art is there for art's
sake; even if Iswall should suggest that in this scene, it would have
to be relativized as expression of his usual one-sidedness. Actually, Iswall
himself feels, when reading silly anecdotes about Dante in a book on
his university's history, that the details of a historical account — and
this holds even more true for a work of art — should be relevant; at
the same time, however, Iswall refuses to accept any doctrinary
simplifications of the "typical" (14–16; 21 f.).

Throughout the *Aula*, humor, wit, and laughing are regarded as deeply
human qualities which relieve the individual from apparent or real
contradictions of life and establish bonds between individuals. The relief
function becomes obvious in an episode dealing with Iswall's visit to
Hamburg. In one scene, he senses particularly intensely the burden of
contradictions in his situation: he, a member of the Socialist Unity Party,
is lying on the couch of his brother-in-law, the "gangster," at the
Reeperbahn in Hamburg, meditating about an activist and a preacher's
daughter and about his former roommates and the name of their room,
"Red October" (115). Iswall overhears a street dialog, and somehow feels

relieved by this: a prostitute proposes to a man who seemingly is on his way home from a tiring night-shift; she claims to be "better than Cleopatra," to which the man retorts "and a bit older, too, I guess" ("Und wohl auch 'n büschen älter!"). This joke is more than an example of a ready-witted answer to an obnoxious advertising slogan; the pattern of the witty retort is ironic acceptance of a hyperbolic statement: although the man refuses the offer, he accepts the woman as a person.

For Iswall this answer becomes symbolic for Hamburg and helps him over is own troubles. It is difficult to name exactly what it is that gives Iswall relief and courage; he may have seen indestructable proletarian optimism, humanity, self-reliance, strength, hope, or courage at the bottom of the man's attitude. What Iswall experiences transcends any narrow psychological or ideological interpretation; he is relieved of ideological worries through the powerful experience of recognition: the man's answer "fitted that city" (116), and Iswall recognizes in the whole street scene a basic pattern of life, a revelation of the human condition.

One notices that Kant does not comment explicitly on the socio-economic aspects of either prostitution or exploitation. At this point, a deep ambivalence in Iswall's — and Kant's — humor becomes apparent: this humor can induce moral strength, but it can also fall short of this goal or even dissipate moral energy by concentrating on Iswall's subjectivity. These considerations may go well beyond literary criticism, but it should be remembered that the theory of Socialist Realism does expect "socialistic impulses" from literature; seen in this context, Kant's humor is an element of balance against too direct a moral appeal, thus becoming the aesthetic conscience of Socialist Realism.

Kant's position within East Germany's emerging Socialism

Marxism claims to be a scientific, critical, and self-critical theory; Kant applies this critical theory to itself. Marx attacks, especially in his early writings, the irrational belief in dogmas; Kant attacks one dogmatism of his times: the irrational and unquestioning belief in what is officially accepted as the correct application of Marx's writings to the situation of East Germany. The situation of East Germany is and was, in marxistic terms, a transitory one. Immediately after the War East Germany passed, according to its own historians, through the phase of transition from fascism to an anti-fascistic-democratic system; since 1949 several stages of the construction of socialism have been declared as having been achieved. But also socialism as a whole is a transitory station on the way to the final goal of history, namely communism. Thus, it is commonplace in East German discussions to say that in their present state of society elements of the old are inextricably intermixed and combined with elements of the new.

Western observers usually go a step further and claim that there is a basic discrepancy between theory and practice in the development of East Germany. If they are marxists, they claim that theory is always ahead of real developments; and if they are not marxists, they argue that there was not a genuine revolution in East Germany after the War, and if there was something like it, it did not live up to the expectations of Walter Ulbricht and other exiles returning from Moscow; yet all changes had to be expressed in terms of this questionable revolution; and that furthermore changes in the Party-line did not necessarily indicate true re-evaluations of previous positions, but instead were frequently results of a power struggle within the Party leadership, if not simply dictates from Moscow.

Kant would obviously accept the framework of a "transitory phase" with respect to the emerging socialism in East Germany; the *Aula* is full of examples of the dialectics of the old and the new. What Kant is concerned with is manipulation and misuse of such concepts. As for the widespread preoccupation with "perspective thinking," with the "orientation towards the future," Kant calls for a sober assessment of the past upon which to base directions for the future. This thought is foreshadowed, backed-up, and, at the same time, understated by the Heine motto even before the narration begins. And looking back into the history of his young country, Kant refuses to believe that Trullesand's marriage and his stay in Peking are simply the work of historical necessity; but in other cases which Kant and his readers may have in mind, such an explanation is indeed given and believed. Kant leaves it open as to whether he is talking about irrationalism or deficiencies restricted to East Germany's early phase, or about ever-present dangers of this kind.

As a critic of irrationalism, Kant is a moralist who tries to enlighten his readers. To do this, Kant has to believe in reason, but this belief is self-critical, intellectualized, and far from naive trust in man's rationality. Hermand mentions, too, that Kant is aware of recurring conflicts caused by imperfections in the human psyche; for him, the "Affe" motif is an acknowledgment of the human *Urseele*.[73]

As for institutions — and the all-important institution is of course the Party as the embodiment of enlightenment — it appears that the powerful Party apparatus indeed infringes upon the rights of the individual in several instances. The unresolved devil metaphor in connection with the scholarship to China seems to hint at the dangers of power, anonymity, hierarchic structure, and pseudo-religious sanctification of marxistic concepts, dangers which are increased and interconnected with the possibility of human emotions such as jealousy.

The treatment of the Russian-Chinese conflict suggests that socialist countries, "where the comrades have won the victory," find themselves faced with unsolvable difficulties, or even outrightly misuse their power by following traditional power politics. As for East Germany's own political and administrative conditions, Kant mentions and alludes to the "Prussian heritage" as one reason for shortcomings in these areas.

One can say that Kant challenges the traditional metaphysical justification of evil; according to this basic pattern of thinking, negative things are the sanctified instrument of, or at least the necessary sacrifice for, the absolute. This line of thought is clearly visible in philosophers of progress like Herder, Hegel, or Marx.

Thus, marxistic apologists have no difficulties in excusing certain shortcomings or problems in their systems; if the "class-enemy" is not called upon as a readily available scapegoat, they minimize and justify the problem in question as a necessary hardship on the thorny road to communism. This was done when Stalin had to explain revocations of progressive enactments in the wake of World War I; and East Germany's official enunciations are still witnessing this kind of argumentation, where restrictions of civic freedom are concerned.

Whereas the "dogmatic" sees, in the final analysis, no real problem in an ethical conflict, Kant does. He regards the relationship between good and evil in a changing society as a rather complex one, as a dilemma for which there is no simple, general answer. Nor does the "dogmatic" see a real problem in the old question of whether the ends justify the means used to achieve them; Kant implies that the means may indeed spoil the ends. If the ends of socialism are served by infringement upon an individual's rights, there is still personal guilt involved, Kant insists, and thus damage done to the society as a whole.

Not only does Kant insist that an evil be recognized and faced as such, but he goes further to question any naive belief that the will of the Party represents automatically and in every instance progress. Is there then a discrepancy between Kant and the Socialist Unity Party of which he is a member? Is Kant actually a revisionist, a counter-revolutionary, or even an anarchist? Kant himself rejected any such allegation emphatically in an article published in the *Neues Deutschland*, after a West German newspaper had interpreted some political comments of his as an indication of a difference between his views and the Party-line.[83] These questions are as controversial as delicate. The best answer would seem to be — and Kant's own article said this in effect — that there cannot be, in principle, any real difference of opinion between the Party and its members since and insofar as the Party stands for everything that is progressive, and since the Party statutes themselves call for self-criticism and courage to tell the truth.

Kant does criticize the literary practices of his country extensively — not to reject them altogether, but in order to promote the truly progressive tendencies in literary life. He is not a liberal in disguise, but claims implicitly to be a better marxist than the literary establishment encourages. And it is because of this loyalty to the cause of socialism that Kant is not satisfied with any cheap, dogmatic harmonization of conflicts within the individual or between the interests of the individual and society. From this follows that Kant cannot advocate just any fashionable, "modern individualism"; if a label must be attached to his position as far as the individual-society conflict is concerned, I would suggest to call it a "new quality of individualism": far removed from any sceptical, egocentric attitude, this individualism requires — in good marxist tradition — insight into some concrete action which will further the cause of socialism. However, it is not the business of some "Big Brother" to enforce this insight upon an individual, but it is the freedom and ultimate responsibility of the individual to bring a sacrifice for the cause — if he so chooses. Thus, history is seen as the result of a complex interconnection of circumstances and actions, many of which are based upon choice; and "historical necessity" is thus reconciled to the dignity of man's free will.[84] This conclusion is based upon an interpretation and extrapolation of the Trullesand episode; the decisive mistake that should not have been made, it seems, is that Trullesand was not given the chance to take the initiative in the decision himself. This freedom was also, in some way or other, denied to Riek who left East Germany.

The theme "Republikflucht," escape from the "Republic," is a traumatic one for most people in East Germany. Kant deals with it at least in four types of cases: there is the unpolitical opportunist who takes as many advantages of the East German system as possible and then leaves to live with relatives in West Germany; there are criminals and perverts who think of the West as their El Dorado; there are people like Fiebach and Iswall's mother who are driven out due to obvious harassment by an individual communist or the administrative apparatus; and, lastly, there are "extreme" cases like that of Riek. Trullesand mentions a similar case to Iswall (449 f.). In the discussion between Trullesand and Iswall, none of the "many question marks" behind the name Riek are answered, and the reader, too, is left without a clear answer as to why persons who seem to be "just right for that country" were lost to it.

Kant's East German critics defend this instance of open-endedness with questionable arguments, or attack it with even more questionable arguments. To claim that it is necessary and good that one specific individual does not always know everything, as the Schlenstedts do concerning Kant's vagueness in this matter, is inconsistent with the *Aula*'s basic principle of all-sided enquiry. The unexplained episode of Riek's leaving East Germany stands out, and it seems as though Kant is sacrificing psychological plausibility for the sake of doing justice to the complex problem of "Republikflucht." The last conclusion about this episode could be that there is an element of tragedy in it, whatever the actual reasons for Riek's going to Hamburg are. Riek is a victim of our times, of the political and social situations in the divided Germany. From this point of view, it does not matter too much whether Riek "actually" fled from East Germany, appalled by the way in which Trullesand and Paal were married and sent to China, or because he tried to escape some secret task offered to him, or because of some other reason; or whether he was more or less forced into an espionage or underground mission which he did carry out, with or without inner enthusiasm.

Another way of describing the overall ideological position is that the novel uses the distinction of evolution and revolution, two aspects inherent in marxism, the former being represented best by the young Marx, the latter by Bolshevist communism. Kant's ridiculing of revolutionary phraseology, his criticism of certain features of stalinism and dogmatism in East Germany (especially in the first years after the War), and the treatment of the idea of "Germany's particular way to socialism," suggest that Kant favors the evolutionary rather than the revolutionary side of socialism: the hardships and hardenings of revolution are the price for the more general process of evolution.

"Having a reason to laugh or smile" is the visible sign of the achievements of Iswall's new society, and in particular of the graduates of the "Workers' and Peasants' College": "Ihnen ist das Grinsen vergangen, und wir lächeln"; ("They've lost their grin; now it is we who are smiling," 361). On the other hand, Party officials like Meibaum are utterly humorless, and therefore more isolated than necessary (cf. 16 f., 260 ff., 395).

It is in keeping with the emphasis on evolution, cooperation, and education that coexistence is seen as more than a tactical manoeuvre: Gropjuhn and Schmöde are accepted as persons (despite their lack of "progressive consciousness"), and there is, at least momentarily on the basis of wit and humor, personal interaction between the "dogmatist" Iswall and the "capitalist" Windshull.

Kant emphasizes the element of humanism in socialism; and if there are terms appropriate for Kant's position, one would have to speak of humanistic socialism, enlightened socialism, or "socialism with a human face," as the term for the recent Czechoslovakian experiment in reform communism is called.[85]

And yet, these attempts here to come to grips with the Aula's message do not fully exhaust the impression projected by the Aula's author. In the chapter on literary references, the frequent quotations from and allusions to Brecht in the Aula were mentioned. These references seem to have deeper significance than just indicating literary or thematic influences: Kant himself has been in somewhat similar situations as Brecht as far as their relationship to the "authorities" is concerned, in that Kant's Impressum was not released until two years after it had been announced and its pre-printing in serial form in a journal was discontinued after a few chapters.[86] The parallels go further: both authors show a preference for the paradox and the parody; and both seem to enjoy, in some aesthetic sense, hiding insurrection against the "powerful ones" behind the appearence of submissiveness. The classical example for this paradoxical attitude is Brecht's appearance before the "American Committee on Unamerican Activities." To be sure, there are differences: Kant got his higher education in East Germany and grew into socialism rather than returned to it from the outside as did Brecht. Yet both Kant and Brecht share the belief in the same truths as the "powerful ones," here the Party; even so, however, the above frictions were possible.

In one East German paper on the *Aula*, Kant is reproached for failing to show that there is an "all-encompassing class-war raging between the worlds of East and West Germany."[87] The reality of class-war is presumably a truth for Kant, but he chooses to concentrate on more difficult truths, namely conflicts within his own society. One such basic conflict which Kant must have experienced should be made explicit: as a Party member, Kant has taken a clear stand for specific Party opinions; but in the *Aula*, he points out the dilemmas of such a position; and as a contributor to the SED daily *Neues Deutschland*, Kant himself uses the simplifications which, in his novels, he avoids or differentiates. The somewhat autobiographical character Iswall experiences similar discrepancies, and it may well be that one of the many facets of the "Affe" motif is the acknowledgment of such role conflicts. Comparable conflicts of roles are probably present in all societies. In the framework of socialistic theory such conflicts can be explained as the "dialectic unity of theory and practice." Again, this argumentation is inly too often a euphemism for a rather mechanical use of the theory, namely as a "manual for revolutionary action." Kant then insists on a deeper, truly dialectical function of literature. Dialectical humor reflects this obvious clash between theory and practice; in the pervasive atmosphere of this humor, unresolved problems are acknowledged as being unresolved, and solutions to conflicts are accepted only as tentative and partial ones.

Form and content in the *Aula* cannot be divorced from one another; and both together are intimately related to issues of what its author regards as the emerging East German socialist society. One the other hand, this novel has many ties to narrative traditions like the educational and humorous novel, traditions which are acknowledged in the novel itself through frequent literary parodies or other references. Thus, it will depend on each reader's standpoint whether to call the *Aula* a high achievement of Socialist Realism or a modern example of Western literary traditions.

The success that the *Aula* has enjoyed in both East and West Germany, as well as in its translations into many European languages, seems well deserved. The interest shown in Kant's novel thus far gives rise to the hope that East Germany will join West Germany in contributing uniquely to world literature, with Hermann Kant's *Aula* being a distinguished achievement of the sixties and a milestone in the development of East German literature as a whole. Beyond this, the success of this novel increases the hope that the societies of the East and West will be able to live together in a spirit of peaceful coexistence — not by forgetting their concrete historical conditions and limitations, but by becoming more aware of their individual strengths and weaknesses; and humor may be an important ingredient in this process.

FOOTNOTES

[1] The quotations are translated from Hans-Dietrich Sander, "*Ideenberatung* mit Walter Ulbricht," in *Deutschland Archiv*, 4 (Cologne, 1971), pp. 422 f.

[2] For details and documentation, see Fritz J. Raddatz, *Traditionen und Tendenzen: Materialien zur Literatur der DDR* (Frankfurt: Suhrkamp, 1972), pp. 383 f.

[3] See Hans-Georg Hölsken, "Zwei Romane: Christa Wolf *Der geteilte Himmel* und Hermann Kant *Die Aula*," in *Deutschunterricht*, 21, No. 5 (Stuttgart: October 1969), pp. 66 f., 72.

[4] See "Der Kampf gegen den Formalismus in Kunst und Literatur für eine fortschrittliche deutsche Kultur," in *Marxismus und Literatur: Eine Dokumentation in drei Bänden*, ed. Fritz J. Raddatz (Reinbek: Rowohlt, 2nd ed. 1971), III, pp. 96–109; cf. also Konrad Franke, *Die Literatur der Deutschen Demokratischen Republik* (Munich and Zurich: Kindler, 1971), pp. 31–39.

[5] See esp. his essay "Über den formalistischen Charakter der Realismustheorie," in *Marxismus und Literatur*, II, pp. 89–94; for an analysis of the controversy between Lukács and Brecht, see Raddatz's preface to his *Marxismus und Literatur*, I, pp. 40–45.

[6] *Die Aula: Roman* (Berlin [East]: Rütten und Loening, 1965), p. 394. Hereafter, simple numbers in the text will refer to pages of this edition. To facilitate the use of the West German hard cover and paperback editions, a page-by-page synopsis of these three editions is provided as appendix to the name index.

[7] See Raddatz, *Traditionen und Tendenzen*, pp. 20–66.

[8] "Auf den Spuren der Wirklichkeit. DDR-Literatur: Traditionen, Tendenzen, Möglichkeiten," in *Deutschunterricht*, 21, No. 5 (Stuttgart, October 1969), pp. 51 f.

[9] Cf. "Modern erzählt: Zu Strukturen in Hermann Kant's Roman *Die Aula*, in *Neue Deutsche Literatur*, 13, No. 12 (Berlin, 1965), p. 15.

[10] Cf. also Hölsken, "Zwei Romane," p. 97.

[11] See Raddatz, *Traditionen und Tendenzen*, pp. 152–157.

[12] "*Die Aula* — Eine Laudatio auf die DDR," in *Kritik in der Zeit: Der Sozialismus — seine Literatur — ihre Entwicklung*, ed. Klaus Jarmatz et. al. (Halle/Saale: Mitteldeutscher Verlag, 1969), pp. 734–742 (rpt. from *Sinn und Form*, 18, No. 1, 1966, pp. 267–273).

[13] Kähler, "*Die Aula*," p. 741; Kähler refers to a review of the *Aula* by Edith Braemer in *Forum*.

[14] in *Weimarer Beiträge*, 12, No. 1 (1966), pp. 15–26.

[15] *Unbequeme Literatur: Eine Beispielreihe*, Literatur und Geschichte. Eine Schriftenreihe, No. 3 (Heidelberg: Stiehm, 1971) pp. 176–192.

[16] "Sozialistisches Biedermeier," in Raddatz, *Traditionen und Tendenzen*, pp. 317–353.

[17] *Traditionen und Tendenzen*, p. 329.

[18] *Traditionen und Tendenzen*, p. 329.

[19] "Modern erzählt," pp. 14 f.

[20] *"Ansichten und Aussichten:* Gespräch mit Autoren," in *Neue Deutsche Literatur,* 14, No. 5 (Berlin, 1966), pp. 36 f.

[21] See 259, 284 f., 300, 389, 412, 415, 427 f., 435; it is ironic that Iswall calls other people "apes" (167).

[22] Cf. the use of the word "Hauptaffe" in a similar scene (427).

[23] Cf. "seiner selbst noch nicht sicher" (not sure of himself yet, 410).

[24] Cf. also "betont selbstbewußt," 248; "Schandmaul," 266; "großes Maul," 428; cf. further 233, 240, 284, 412, 452.

[25] *Ein bißchen Südsee: Erzählungen* (Munich: dtv No. 679, 1970), pp. 110–119; see especially "Hochmutsfimmel," "Angeberei," "Angeber," "arrogantes Zeug," pp. 118 f.

[26] Cf. further 106, 417 f.

[27] *Unbequeme Literatur,* p. 181.

[28] Cf. also "Du weißt ja, wie das damals war," 354.

[29] The word "Bewußtsein" (consciousness) has undergone a change of meaning in East German usage, substituting for "richtiges Bewußtsein" or "Klassenbewußtsein."

[30] Cf. the interviews contained in Barbara Grunert-Bronnen, *Ich bin Bürger der DDR und lebe in der Bundesrepublik* (Munich: Piper, 1970).

[31] *Nachdenken über Christa T.* (Berlin: Luchterhand, 1969; trans. under the title "Quest for Christa T."), pp. 127 ff.

[32] Cf. also "die andere [Lehrerin an der polnischen Antifa-Schule, T. L.] behauptete, der Mensch verliere erst seinen Affenschwanz, wenn er das *Kapital* verstanden habe," 251; elsewhere, apes are humorously contrasted with human beings: apes are able to throw rocks into the air and watch them fall, but they are unable to calculate this phenomenon, 322.

[33] *Thus Spake Zarathustra,* trans. Thomas Common (New. York: Russel, 1964), pp. 6 f.

[34] *Marxismus und das menschliche Individuum,* rowohlts deutsche enzyklopädie, No. 332 (Reinbek: Rowohlt, 1970).

[35] *Die Deutsche Ideologie,* in *Marx-Engels-Gesamtausgabe,* I, 5, p. 59; quoted from Adam Schaff, *Marxismus und das menschliche Individuum,* p. 87.

[36] Cf. also "Ein deutscher Kopfmensch. Aber noch immer kein Mensch," Bernhard Seeger, "Fiete Stein," in *Neue Deutsche Literatur,* 18, No. 2 (1970), p. 66.

[37] See 173, 176, 196, 200, 357, 377 ff.

[38] Cf. further "beschnuppern," 34; "beäugen," "aufpassen ... wie ein Schießhund," 59; "anäugen," 274; "Elephantenknie," 369; "wie ein besonders treues Kaninchen," 375; "sich beäugen lassen," 416; "ich Esel," 427; "zwitschern," 444; "der Wagen ... senkte die Lichthörner und war ein Stier," 463.

[39] Erwin Strittmatter, *Ole Bienkopp,* (Berlin, 1963), p. 319.

[40] Alexander Solschenizyn, *Ein Tag im Leben des Iwan Denissowitsch* (Gütersloh: Mohn, n. d.), pp. 62 ff.; cf. also a reference to this "regulation" p. 67.

[41] See above p. 32.

[42] Cf. also "Die Frage ist eine politische." (The question is a political one.) and "politisch gesehen" (from a political point of view), 158 f.

[43] Cf. further "so gehe denn hin und zahle es ihm heim mit guten Taten, gehe hin und mehre den Wald ...," 366 f; "denn siehe, in einer jeglichen Nacht" 255;

the archaic comparative conjunction "denn" is used instead of the usual "als" or the colloquial "wie," 116.

[44] Cf. further "der fromme Herr" 44; "Herr Seelsorger," "Fräulein Pastor" 45; "Bibelforscher aus dem Mittelalter" 71; "Die reinste Jesuitenschule".... "Nein, es gibt eine Sekte, die heißen Herrnhuter, das sind besonders Fromme, und was die da aufhaben, das ist ihr Sektenzeichen, der Herrnhuterhut!" 78; "Ich hatte gedacht, das gibt einen jesuitischen Jiu-Jitsu-Kampf, aber der Pope ging aus wie ein Kirchenlicht." 400.

[45] Neubert, "Komisches und Satirisches," p. 23.

[46] Neubert, "Komisches und Satirisches," p. 20.

[47] See 203 ff., 251, 281, 297, 401 f.

[48] Schlenstedt, "Modern erzählt," p. 15.

[49] For a detailed discussion of this question see Raddatz *Traditionen und Tendenzen*, pp. 460 ff.; cf. also Schlenstedt, "Modern erzählt," p. 24.

[50] Carola Stern, *Ulbricht: A Political Biography* (New York, 1965), p. 17.

[51] Cf. above p. 19.

[52] *Birth of the Communist Manifesto*, ed. Dirk J. Struik (New York: International Publishers, 1971), p. 31.

[53] "Modern erzählt," p. 24.

[54] See above p. 42.

[55] Cf. John Flores, *Poetry in East Germany*, p. 12.

[56] Cf. especially 70, 277 f.; cf. further 107 ff., 283 ff., 303, 370 f.

[57] The author is unable to locate the source of these quotes; it is possible that Kant made them up.

[58] "Die Aula," ed. Deutsches Theater/Kammerspiele (Berlin, February 1969), esp. p. 13.

[59] Cf. also John Flores, *Poetry in East Germany*, pp. 6 ff.

[60] See Frank Trommler, "Von Stalin zu Hölderlin," in *Basis*, 2 (Frankfurt: Athenäum, 1971), p. 181 f.

[61] Quoted from Dieter Schlenstedt, "Ankunft und Anspruch," in *Sinn und Form*, 13, No. 3, pp. 818 f.

[62] For a detailed comparison of the storm motif in Schulz and in Immermann, see Frank Trommler, "Von Stalin zu Hölderlin," pp. 177 f.

[63] *Ole Bienkopp*, p. 76.

[64] Cf. above p. 69 in the section on religious language.

[65] in *Sinn und Form*, 1 and 2 (1965).

[66] Hermand (*Unbequeme Literatur*, p. 190) mentions that Neutsch uses this very poem as the motto for his novel *Die Spur der Steine*.

[67] *Poetry in East Germany*, esp. pp. 275 ff.

[68] *Der Spiegel* XVI, No. 37 (September 12, 1962), p. 54; quoted from D. L. Ashliman, Popular Culture in Foreign-Language Curricula," in *Die Unterrichtspraxis*, 4, No. 1 (Spring 1971), p. 74.

[69] *The Return of the Vanishing American* (New York, 1968), p. 77; quoted from D. L. Ashliman, "Popular Culture in Foreign-Language Curricula," in *Die Unterrichtspraxis*, 4, No. 1 (Spring 1971), p. 74.

[70] Hermand (*Unbequeme Literatur*, pp. 190 f.) also noted this critical tone.

[71] For details, see Raddatz, *Traditionen und Tendenzen*, pp. 438 ff., as well as the pertinent essays in *Marxismus und Literatur*, especially Ernst Fischer, "Doktor Faustus und der deutsche Bauernkrieg," III, pp. 110-122.

[72] Charles West, *Communism and the Theologians* (New York: MacMillan, 1958), p. 93.

[73] *Unbequeme Literatur*, p. 189.

[74] *Das Impressum*, p. 235, p. 248.

[75] "Modern erzählt," p. 33.

[76] "Modern erzählt," pp. 30 ff.

[77] "Modern erzählt," pp. 31 f.

[78] "Modern erzählt," p. 34.

[79] "Modern erzählt," pp. 15 ff.

[80] "Modern erzählt," pp. 19 f.

[81] *Unbequeme Literatur*, p. 180.

[82] "Modern erzählt," p. 32.

[83] "Auskunft an Bedürftige," in *Neues Deutschland*, 9 November 1969; rprt. in Konrad Franke, *Die Literatur der Deutschen Demokratischen Republik*, pp. 360 f.

[84] About this problem, cf. also Ernst Fischer, *Auf den Spuren der Wirklichkeit* (Hamburg, 1968), p. 225.

[85] Hölsken ("Zwei Romane," pp. 69 ff.) tries to link Kant to intracommunist opposition.

[86] See Franke, *Die Literatur der Deutschen Demokratischen Republik*, p. 350, and Raddatz, *Traditionen und Tendenzen*, p. 570.

[87] Kähler, "Die Aula," p. 741.

SELECTED BIBLIOGRAPHY

I. Primary Literature

KANT, HERMANN. Die Aula: Roman. Berlin [East]: Rütten und Loening, 1965.

—. Die Aula: Roman. Munich: Rütten und Loening, 1965.

—. Ein bißchen Südsee: Erzählungen. Munich: dtv No. 679, 1970.

—. Das Impressum: Roman. Berlin [East]: Rütten und Leoning, 1972.

SOLSCHENIZYN, ALEXANDER. Ein Tag im Leben des Iwan Dennissowitsch: Erzählung. Tr. W. Löser and others. Gütersloh: Mohn, n. y.

STRITTMATTER, ERWIN. Ole Bienkopp. Berlin, 1963.

WOLF, CHRISTA. Der geteilte Himmel. Halle/Saale: Mitteldeutscher Verlag, 1963.

—. Nachdenken über Christa T. Halle/Saale: Mitteldeutscher Verlag, 1968.

II. Secondary Literature

BILKE, JÖRG BERNHARD. "Auf den Spuren der Wirklichkeit: DDR-Literatur — Traditionen, Tendenzen, Möglichkeiten." Deutschunterricht, 21, No. 5 (October 1969), pp. 24-60.

FISCHER, ERNST. Auf den Spuren der Wirklichkeit. Hamburg, 1968.

—. Kunst und Koexistenz: Beitrag zu einer modernen marxistischen Ästhetik. Reinbek: Rowohlt, 1966.

FLORES, JOHN. Poetry in East Germany: Adjustments, Visions, Provocations, 1945-1970. Yale Germanic Studies, No. 5. New Haven and London: Yale University Press, 1971.

FRANKE, KONRAD. Die Literatur der Deutschen Demokratischen Republik. Kindlers Literaturgeschichte der Gegenwart in Einzelbänden. Munich and Zurich: Kindler, 1971.

HERMAND, JOST. "Hermann Kant: Die Aula." Unbequeme Literatur: Eine Beispielreihe. Literatur und Geschichte, No. 5. Heidelberg: Lothar Stiehm, 1971, pp. 176-213.

HÖLSKEN, HANS GEORG. "Zwei Romane: Christa Wolf 'Der geteilte Himmel' und Hermann Kant 'Die Aula.' " Deutschunterricht, 21, No. 5 (Oct. 1969), pp. 61-99.

KÄHLER, HERMANN. " 'Die Aula' — eine Laudatio auf die DDR." Kritik in der Zeit. Ed. Klaus Jarmatz and others. Halle/Saale: Mitteldeutscher Verlag, 1969. pp. 734-42.

KANT, HERMANN [and others]. "Ansichten und Aussichten: Gespräch mit Autoren." Neue Deutsche Literatur, 14, No. 5 (1966), pp. 18–42.

MARXISMUS UND LITERATUR: Eine Dokumentation in drei Bänden. Ed. Fritz J. Raddatz. Rowohlt Paperback, No. 80–82. 2nd ed. Reinbek: Rowohlt, 1971.

NEUBERT, WERNER. "Komisches und Satirisches in Hermann Kants 'Aula'" Weimarer Beiträge, 12, No. 1 (1966), pp. 15–26.

RADDATZ, FRITZ: Traditionen und Tendenzen: Materialien zur Literatur der DDR. Frankfurt: Suhrkamp, 1972.

SCHAFF, ADAM. Marxismus und das menschliche Individuum. rowohlts deutsche encyklopädie, No. 332. Reinbek: Rowohlt, 1970.

SCHLENSTEDT, SILVIA AND DIETER. "Modern erzählt: Zu Strukturen in Hermann Kants Roman 'Die Aula.'" Neue Deutsche Literatur, 13, No. 12 (1965), pp. 5–34.

INDEX

78, 82–86, 88–93, 103, 108–115
German Writers' Union, 34, 88, 100, 103
Germany: *See* Federal Republic of Germany; German Democratic Republic
Goethe, Johann Wolfgang, 44, 92; *Faust,* 57, 95; "Prometheus," 94
Gorki, Maxim, 99
Gottfried von Straßburg: *Tristan und Isolde,* 95
Grass, Günter, 18
Greece: Athenian eloquence, 105; Thucydides, 76
Grunert-Bronnen, Barbara, 25 (n. 30)
Gulbranssen, Trygve: *Und ewig singen die Wälder,* 83

Hamburg, 65, 69, 97, 107 f., 112; Reeperbahn, 32, 61, 107
Havemann, Robert, 9, 68
Hegel, Georg Wilhelm Friedrich, 37, 110
Heine, Heinrich, 21, 90, 96 f., 109; "Deutschland. Ein Wintermärchen," 7, 90, 97; *Ideen. Das Buch Le Grand,* 97 f.
Herder, Johann Gottfried, 110
Hermand, Jost: *Unbequeme Literatur,* 9, 22, 90 (n. 66), 98, 104 (n. 81), 109 f., 120
Hermlin, Stephan: "Die Kommandeuse," 7
Herwegh, Georg: "Bundeslied," 87
Heyse, Paul von, 100
Hitler, Adolf, 5
Hölderlin, Friedrich, 83
Hölsken, Hans-Georg, 4 (n. 3), 7 (n. 10), 9, 113 (n. 85), 120
Homer, 39
Humor, 9, 12, 18 f., 34, 38, 45 f., 56, 59, 67, 75, 78, 97, 107 f., 113, 115; dialectical humor, 10, 13, 22, 28–31, 34, 43, 47, 51, 71, 73, 98 f., 101–104, 106, 114; humorous, 16 f., 24, 30, 32, 34–36, 39 f., 43, 50, 54, 61, 63, 74 f., 77–79, 88, 98, 103, 106

Immermann, Karl: *Die Epigonen,* 84
Internationale (song), 67
Irony, 9, 11 f., 18 f., 24 f., 35, 47, 58, 62, 65–67, 69, 73, 79; epic irony, 102 f.; ironic(al), 15, 17–19, 30, 36, 39, 45, 54, 56, 58, 62, 64 f., 69 f., 72 f., 77, 84–86, 108; ironize, 37, 39, 46 f., 48, 52, 54, 69, 78

Jesus, 53, 61, 65, 71 f.

Kafka, Franz, 88, 98; Kafka Conference (Liblice/Prague, 1963), 27
Kähler, Hermann, 8, 114 (n. 87)
Kant, Hermann: "Ansichten und Aussichten," 13 (n. 20), 121; *Die Aula,* pass.; "Die Aula" (theater version), 14, 79; "Auskunft an Bedürftige," 111 (n. 83); *Das Impressum,* 2, 6 f., 10, 19, 98, 113; "Die Werbung," 19
Keller, Gottfried: "Abendlied," 43, 61, 78, 93 f.
Kunert, Günter, 7

Laplace, Pierre Simon de, 68
Latin, 38 f., 52, 62; the Romans, 80
Leipzig: Leipzig Fair, 11
Lemmer, Ernst, 10
Lenin, Vladimir I., 22, 64, 83; leninism, 3; leninist, 3 f., 80, 101
Lessing, Gotthold Ephraim, 28
Literature: Classical (German) 39, 83, 92–98; Middle High German, 63; trivial, 42, 91 f.
Lukács, Georg, 5
Luther, Martin, 19, 49, 53 f., 57–60, 65, 95 f.; "Wider die räuberischen und mörderischen Rotten der Bauern," 59 f.

Mann, Thomas, 92; *Doktor Faustus,* 57, 95
Mao Tse Tung: Maoist, 80
Marx, Karl, 22, 26 f., 64, 80, 108, 110, 112; marxism, 3 f., 19, 28, 46, 64, 80, 108, 112; marxist, 5, 43, 45 f., 51, 59,

APPENDIX

Pagination concordance of *Aula* editions

A East German hardback edition (Berlin [East]: Rütten und Loening, 1965)
B West German hardback edition (Munich: Rütten und Loening, 1965)
C West German paperback edition (Frankfurt: Fischer [No. 931], 1968)

A	B	C	A	B	C
7	7	7	39	34–5	28–9
8	7–8	7–8	40	35–6	29
9	8–9	8–9	41	36–7	29–30
10	9–10	9	42	37–8	30–1
11	10–1	9–10	43	38–9	31
12	11–2	10–1	44	39–40	32
13	12–3	11	45	40	32–3
14	13–4	11–2	46	40–1	33
15	14	12–3	47	41–2	33–4
16	14–5	13	48	42–3	34–5
17	15–6	13–4	49	43–4	35
18	16–7	14–5	50	44–5	35–6
19	17–8	15	51	45–6	36–7
20	18–9	15–6	52	46–7	37–8
21	19–20	16–7	53	47–8	38
22	20	17	54	48	38–9
23	20–1	17–8	55	48–9	39–40
24	21–2	18–9	56	49–50	40
25	22–3	19	57	50–1	40–1
26	23–4	19–20	58	51–2	41–2
27	24–5	20–1	59	52–3	42
28	25–6	21	60	53–4	42–3
29	26–7	21–2	61	54	43–4
30	27	22–3	62	54–5	44
31	27–8	23	63	55–6	44–5
32	28–9	23–4	64	56–7	45–6
33	29–30	24–5	65	57–8	46
34	30–1	25	66	58–9	46–7
35	31–2	26	67	59–60	47–8
36	32–3	26–7	68	60	48
37	33	27	69	60–1	48–9
38	33–4	27–8	70	61–2	49–50

A	B	C	A	B	C
71	62–3	50	115	101–2	80
72	63–4	50–1	116	102–3	80–1
73	64–5	51–2	117	103–4	81–2
74	65–6	52	118	104	82
75	66	52–3	119	104–5	82–3
76	66–7	53–4	120	105–6	83–4
77	67–8	54	121	106–7	84–5
78	68–9	54–5	122	107–8	85
79	69–70	55–6	123	108–9	85–6
80	70–1	56–7	124	109–10	86–7
81	71–2	57	125	110–1	87
82	72–3	57–8	126	111–2	87–8
83	73–4	58–9	127	112	88–9
84	74	59	128	112–3	89
85	74–5	59–60	129	113–4	89–90
86	75–6	60–1	130	114–5	90–1
87	76–7	61	131	115–6	91
88	77–8	61–2	132	116–7	91–2
89	78–9	62–3	133	117–8	92–3
90	79–80	63	134	118–9	93
91	80–1	63–4	135	119	93–4
92	81–2	64–5	136	119–20	94–5
93	82	65	137	120–1	95–6
94	83	65–6	138	121–2	96
95	83–4	66–7	139	122–3	96–7
96	84–5	67	140	123–4	97–8
97	85–6	67–8	141	124–5	98
98	86–7	68–9	142	125–6	98–9
99	87–8	69	143	126	99–100
100	88–9	69–70	144	127–7	100
101	89	70–1	145	127–8	100–1
102	89–90	71	146	128–9	101–2
103	90–1	72	147	129–30	102
104	91–2	72–3	148	130–1	102–3
105	92–3	73–4	149	131–2	103–4
106	93–4	74	150	132–3	104
107	94–5	74–5	151	133–4	104–5
108	95–6	75–6	152	134	105–6
109	96	76	153	134–5	106
110	97	76–7	154	135–6	106–7
111	97 8	77–8	155	136–7	107–8
112	98–9	78	156	137–8	108–9
113	99–100	78–9	157	138–9	109
114	100–1	79–80	158	139–40	109–10

A	B	C	A	B	C
159	140–1	110–1	203	178–9	140
160	141	111	204	179–80	140–1
161	141–2	111–2	205	180–1	141–2
162	142–3	112–3	206	181–2	142
163	143–4	113	207	182	142–3
164	144–5	113–4	208	182–3	143–4
165	145–6	114–5	209	183–4	144–5
166	146–7	115	210	184–5	145
167	147	115–6	211	185–6	145–6
168	147–8	116	212	186–7	156–7
169	148–9	117	213	187–8	147
170	140–50	117–8	214	188	147–8
171	150–1	118–9	215	189	148–9
172	151–2	119	216	189–90	149
173	152–3	119–20	217	190–1	149–50
174	153–4	120–1	218	191–2	150–1
175	154	121	219	192–3	151
176	154–5	121–2	220	193–4	151–2
177	155–6	122–3	221	194–5	152–3
178	156–7	123	222	195	153
179	157–8	123–4	223	195–6	153–4
180	158–9	124–5	224	196–7	154–5
181	159–60	125	225	197–8	155
182	160	125–6	226	198–9	155–6
183	161	126–7	227	199–200	156–7
184	161–3	127	228	200–1	157
185	162–3	127–8	229	201	157–8
186	163–4	128–9	230	201–2	158–9
187	164–5	129	231	202–3	159
188	165–6	129–30	232	203–4	159–60
189	166–7	130–1	233	204–5	160–1
190	167–8	131	234	205–6	161
191	168	131–2	235	206–7	161–2
192	168–9	132–3	236	207–8	162–3
193	169–70	133	237	208	163–4
194	170–1	134	238	208–9	164
195	171–2	134–5	239	209–10	164–5
196	172–3	135–6	240	210–1	165–6
197	173–4	136	241	211–2	166
198	174–5	136–7	242	212–3	166–7
199	175–6	137–8	243	213–4	167–8
200	176	138	244	214–5	168
201	176–7	138–9	245	215	168–9
202	177–8	139–40	246	216	169–70

A	B	C	A	B	C
247	216-7	170-1	291	255	199-200
248	217-8	171	292	255-6	200-1
249	218-9	171-2	293	256-7	201
250	219-20	172-3	294	257-8	201-2
251	220-1	173	295	258-9	202-3
252	221-2	173-4	296	259-60	203
253	222-3	174-5	297	260-1	203-4
254	223	175	298	261	204-5
255	223-4	175-6	299	261-2	205
256	224-5	176-7	300	262-3	205-6
257	225-6	177	301	263-4	206-7
258	226-7	177-8	302	264-5	207-8
259	227-8	178	303	265-6	208
260	228-9	178-9	304	266-7	208-9
261	229	179-80	305	267-8	209-10
262	229-30	180	306	268	210
263	230-1	180-1	307	269	210-1
264	231-2	181-2	308	269-70	211-2
265	232-3	182	309	270-1	212
266	233-4	182-3	310	271-2	212-3
267	234-5	183-4	311	272-3	213-4
268	235	184-5	312	273-4	214
269	235-6	185	313	274-5	214-5
270	236-7	185-6	314	275	215-6
271	237-8	186-7	315	275-6	216
272	238-9	187	316	276-7	216-7
273	239-40	187-8	317	277-8	217-8
274	240-1	188-9	318	278-9	218
275	241-2	189	319	279-80	218-9
276	242	189-90	320	280-1	219-20
277	242-3	190-1	321	281	220
278	243-4	191	322	282	220-1
279	244-5	191-2	323	282-3	221-2
280	245-6	192-3	324	283-4	222
281	246-7	193	325	284-5	222-3
282	247-8	193-4	326	285-6	223-4
283	248	194-5	327	286-7	224-5
284	248-9	195	328	287	225
285	249-50	195-6	329	228	225-6
286	251-2	196-7	330	288-9	226-7
287	252-3	197	331	289-90	227
288	253-4	197-8	332	290-1	227-8
289	254-5	198-9	333	291-2	228-9
290	254	199	334	292-3	229

A	B	C	A	B	C
335	293–4	229–30	379	331–2	259–60
336	294–5	230–1	380	332–3	260
337	295	231	381	333–4	260–1
338	295–6	231–2	382	334–5	261–2
339	296–7	232–3	383	335–6	262
340	297–8	233	384	336–7	262–3
341	298–9	233–4	385	337	263–4
342	299–300	234–5	386	337–8	264
343	300–1	235	387	338–9	264–5
344	301–2	235–6	388	339–40	265–6
345	302	236–7	389	340–1	266
346	302–3	237	390	341–2	266–7
347	303–4	237–8	391	342–3	267–8
348	304–5	238–9	392	343–4	268–9
349	305–6	239–40	393	344	269
350	306–7	240	394	344–5	269–70
351	307–8	240–1	395	345–6	270–1
352	308–9	241–2	396	346–7	271
353	309–10	242	397	347–8	271–2
354	310	242–3	398	348–9	272–3
355	310–1	243–4	399	349–50	273
356	311–2	244	400	350	273–4
357	312–3	244–5	401	351	274–5
358	313–4	245–6	402	351–2	275
359	314–5	246	403	352–3	275–6
360	315–6	246–7	404	253–4	276–7
361	316	247–8	405	354–5	277
362	316–7	248	406	355–6	277–8
363	317–8	248–9	407	356–7	278–9
364	318–9	249–50	408	357	279
365	319–20	250	409	357–8	279–80
366	320–1	250–1	410	358–9	280–1
367	321–2	251–2	411	359–60	281
368	322–3	252	412	360–1	281–2
369	323	252–3	413	361–2	282–3
370	323–4	253–4	414	362–3	283
371	324–5	254	415	363	283–4
372	325–6	254–5	416	364	284–5
373	326–7	255–6	417	364–5	285
374	327–8	256	418	365–6	285–6
375	328–9	256–7	419	366–7	286–7
376	329–30	257–8	420	367–8	287
377	330	258	421	368–9	287–8
378	330–1	258–9	422	369–70	288–9

A	B	C	A	B	C
423	370-1	289	444	388-9	303
424	371	289-90	445	389-90	303-4
425	371-2	290-1	446	390	304-5
426	372-3	291	447	391	305-6
427	373-4	291-2	448	391-2	306
428	374-5	292-3	449	392-3	306-7
429	375-6	293	450	393-4	307-8
430	376-7	293-4	451	394-5	308
431	377-8	294-5	452	395-6	308-9
432	378	295	453	396-7	309-10
433	378-9	295-6	454	397	310
434	379-80	296-7	455	397-8	310-1
435	380-1	297	456	398-9	311-2
436	381-2	297-8	457	399-400	312
437	382-3	298-9	458	400-1	312-3
438	383-4	299	459	401-2	313-4
439	384	299-300	460	402-3	314
440	385	300-1	461	403-4	314-5
441	385-6	301	462	404-5	315-6
442	386-7	302	463	405	316
443	387-8	302-3	464	405-6	316-7

HOLGER A. PAUSCH (Hrsg.)
Kommunikative Metaphorik — Studien zur Funktion des literarischen Bildes in der deutschen Literatur von den Anfängen bis zur Gegenwart
ca. 280 S., kart. ca. DM 29,—; ISBN 3 416 01013 2
Studien zur Germanistik, Anglistik und Komparatistik, Band 20

HARRO MÜLLER
Theodor Storms Lyrik
ca. 190 S., kart. ca. DM 29,—; ISBN 3 416 01017 5
Literatur und Wirklichkeit, Band 13

DAVID G. RICHARDS
Georg Büchners „Woyzeck" — Interpretation und Textgestaltung
ca. 65 S., kart. ca. DM 12,—; ISBN 3 416 01057 4
Abhandlungen zur Kunst-, Musik- und Literaturwissenschaft, Band 188

HEINRICH RICHARTZ
Literaturkritik als Gesellschaftskritik — Darstellungsweise und politisch-didaktische Intention in Gottfried Kellers Erzählkunst
284 S., kart. DM 48,—; ISBN 3 416 01035 3
Abhandlungen zur Kunst-, Musik- und Literaturwissenschaft, Band 159

PETER RICHTER
Franz Kafka — Variation als Prinzip in seinen Romanen
X, 367 S., kart. DM 68,—; ISBN 3 416 01009 4
Abhandlungen zur Kunst-, Musik- und Literaturwissenschaft, Band 166

RENA R. SCHLEIN
Ritterlichkeit — Fragment aus dem Nachlaß Arthur Schnitzlers
ca. 120 S., kart. ca. DM 19,—; ISBN 3 416 01056 6
Abhandlungen zur Kunst-, Musik- und Literaturwissenschaft, Band 176

ALFRED SCHMIDT
Wolfgang Borchert — Sprachgestaltung in seinem Werk
VI, 322 S., kart. DM 48,—; ISBN 3 416 01085 X
Abhandlungen zur Kunst-, Musik- und Literaturwissenschaft, Band 186

JENS STÜBEN
Parteilichkeit — Zur Kritik der marxistischen Literaturtheorie
134 S., kart. DM 22,—; ISBN 3 416 01041 8
Abhandlungen zur Kunst-, Musik- und Literaturwissenschaft, Band 171

FRANK W. YOUNG
Montage and Motif in Thomas Mann's, "Tristan"
VI, 142 S., kart. DM 124,—; ISBN 3 416 01082 5
Abhandlungen zur Kunst-, Musik- und Literaturwissenschaft, Band 183

BOUVIER VERLAG HERBERT GRUNDMANN · BONN